When You Give Joy, You Get Joy Back

Expressions of Love for Meadowlark

"The Globetrotters made a lot of friends over the years – in towns and cities all over the world – and made basketball fans out of people who didn't have any idea what basketball was. I first met Mead in North Carolina. I put him in a uniform that very night and he even got to play a little. He had a lot of confidence in what his intentions were. I told Abe (Saperstein) about him. I said, "That is a future Globetrotter." He was already a good athlete. He made himself a natural comedian. He wanted to do the comedy routines. He did that through hard work, through concentration, and he applied himself. Without self-application, you never can do it. He saw something he wanted to do – a role he wanted to play – the comedy routines. He worked hard, and he accomplished what he wanted. Now, he's not only a good basketball player, but a self-made comedian.

People liked him and enjoyed him and came back to see him over and over, and this has been going on for years."

> – Marques Haynes, the legendary Globetrotter who gave
> Meadowlark his tryout with the team, HOF 1998

◆

"I enjoyed playing with Meadowlark for 15 years with the Globetrotters. We played over 6,000 games together all over the world. He's an inspiration to me and I learned a lot from him. He's one of the greatest showmen that ever played for the Globetrotters, right up there with 'Goose' Tatum and 'Geese' Ausbie. He's always been a great friend and motivator for me.

All I think about are the good times with Meadowlark and fond memories of the two of us and the rest of the teammates, the joy of giving back to people and children all over the world.

The Globetrotters are one of the greatest basketball teams of all time. They gave Meadowlark and me a chance to perfect our basketball skills and showcase them all over the world. We want to thank Abe Saperstein and his family, and the Harlem Globetrotters."

> – Curly Neal, the famous ball-handling showman of the Harlem Globetrotters

◆

"Meadowlark Lemon is one very clever man, unique and truly one of a kind."

> – Mickey Rooney, beloved actor and comedian

◆

"To know him is to truly love him He's an extremely nice man. I'm glad that we were inducted in the same class at the Hall of Fame (2003). The man is a true icon ... Meadow is the kind of guy who would never have a bad night plying his craft. If you thought enough of him to pay to come and see him play, you truly got entertained."

> – Earl Lloyd, first African-American to play in the NBA, HOF 2003

"It is my honor and pleasure to be included in my 'big brother' Meadowlark Lemon's book.

I am the daughter of Abe Saperstein, the founder and coach of the Harlem Globetrotters. We were raised as one big family, so I am very lucky to have a lot of big brothers!

How I remember that warm summer evening in Germany in the late 1950s. "Goose" Tatum had left the Globetrotters along with Marques Haynes to form their own team in 1952. My father kept looking for the ideal person to be 'the Clown Prince of Basketball.' No one seemed to fill the criteria my father had in his mind. Not until that warm evening ... I was sitting next to my dad when this young soldier came over to us and introduced himself. 'I'm Meadow Lemon.' My dad and he spoke for a short time. Meadow then walked on. My father said to me he had seen Meadow play in the U.S. and then said, 'Honey girl, you just met the future star of the Harlem Globetrotters!' And how true that was for all those years!"

– Eloise Saperstein, daughter of Globetrotters' Founder Abe Saperstein

♦

"Meadowlark and I have been friends for more than 50 years. When we were in high school, my team was probably the No.1 team in the state of North Carolina. His school, Williston High School, was probably the second best in the state, so it was always a challenge every time we had to compete against each other. Because of our relationship, I look for him at every golf tournament and event I appear at across the country. We have such a good time together. We grew up together, we are great friends, and we continue to be so."

– Sam Jones, legendary NBA All Star, HOF 1984

♦

"We roomed together for the first 12 years Meadowlark played with us. He's one of the most dedicated Globetrotters I've ever been around. His primary objective every time he hit the floor was to make people happy, and make them have one of the greatest experiences of their lifetime. That was embedded in him. That's all he thought about."

– Charles "Tex" Harrison, coach and former player of the Harlem Globetrotters

♦

"Mr. Lemon-Man has inspired millions across the world through his gift. I don't refer only to basketball, but also to his magnificent gift of caring, sharing, and loving all people. I only hope my kids would possess an ounce of the Lemon-Man's heart, which easily radiates through that smile."

– A.C. Green, Los Angeles Laker great, aka Ironman
Founder, A.C. Green Youth Foundation

♦

"Meadowlark inspired me to play for a long time. I thought, 'If he could do it, I can do it.' The legacy that Meadowlark leaves is something that every child and adult can benefit from."

– Robert Parish, Boston Celtics great, HOF 2003

"Meadowlark always amazed me because of his rapport with the crowds that came out to see the Globetrotters. He is the funniest guy in the world. The character that he played – that's his personality! He makes people laugh and open to receive the joy he brings with him. I love that guy.

I'm so proud of him. God took him from being lost to finding a great wife and family.

I'm glad he's sharing his life story. He is a precious person. We are all precious and valuable and unique. That skill that you have – you already have the skills to make it in this world – that's the way God planned it. All you have to do is develop them.

`When we talk on the phone – before we even start talking – we are laughing."

> – Rosey Grier, former NFL All-Pro Defensive Tackle,
> member of the Fearsome Foursome

♦

"When I was nine years old, I saw Meadowlark Lemon and the Globetrotters play for the first time on television, on ABC's Wide World of Sports. He mesmerized me with his antics and I could not move from that television. After the game, I ran to my mom and said, 'Mom, I want to become a Globetrotter just like Meadowlark Lemon.' So I wrote it down on a piece of paper. That piece of paper reminded me to do all of the necessary things throughout my life in order to reach that goal. In 1985, I got that chance to play for the world-famous Harlem Globetrotters. That dream lasted for 11 years.

Now I've known Meadowlark (Youngfella) Lemon for over a decade and he has been a father, a friend, and a mentor to me. Before playing with Meadowlark, I'd never had an opportunity to play with such a perfectionist. He is touched by GOD to bring joy and happiness to others and to put smiles on the faces of the young and the young at heart. Love you!

> – Tyrone "Hollywood" Brown, former Harlem Globetrotter
> and current member of Meadowlark Lemon's Harlem All Stars™

♦

"Wonders never cease is the only way to explain the phenomenon of how extraordinary talent befalls certain individuals. These phenomena are called miracles. No one can explain Meadowlark Lemon's beginning or how he developed the ability to captivate the world and make them forget about their troubles, wars, and tribulations. There will never be another. There is no account of any other close to him. I lived to be able to call one of God's miracles my friend, confidant, and mentor. He is not the Clown Prince, but the 'Crowned Prince' of basketball."

> – Les "Pee Wee" Harrison, 24-year running mate and current
> member of Meadowlark Lemon's Harlem All Stars™

♦

"The word came to us at Trinity Broadcast Network (TBN) in 1982 that 'the' Meadowlark Lemon was born again. We could not even dream that this legend would grace our little TV station. But one day, bigger than life, he walked in with a grin from ear to ear and a heart as big as a basketball and a spirit that would melt your soul.

It was love at first sight, and second and third, and until this day.

I remember inviting Meadowlark to Raleigh, North Carolina, for a TBN family rally. We were staying in a hotel there and we were to meet in the lobby at 5 o'clock to ride to the auditorium together. We heard there was a huge group of teenagers celebrating their graduation from high school but thought 'they won't know us, so we'll just go right through the crowd.'

All of a sudden, I heard screaming and shouting and running toward our group.

I thought 'ohhhhh no, they know us and we'll be late,' but all I could see was bodies running past me and screaming 'Meadowlark, Meadowlark, Meadowlark Lemon!'

They jumped and screamed and got autographs and pictures for 30 minutes.

In the meantime, I was standing close by just holding his coat and Bible. He was gracious to all of them.

I think in the end I said, 'Sir, can I have your autograph, too?' I probably still have it somewhere to this day. After all, it's Meadowlark Lemon, people! *The* Meadowlark Lemon! Now, get me this book. I can't wait to read it. I wonder if he'd autograph one for me – 'Oh, I hope so!' Make it out to: 'Your best friend on earth, Jan Crouch,' please?? I wanna show it to my grandchildren. They'll think Gramma's cool."

– Jan Crouch, Founder, Trinity Broadcasting Network (TBN)
Founder, Smile of a Child Foundation

♦

"Meadowlark Lemon is the most popular Harlem Globetrotter who ever played. He is truly an icon who made history in basketball and deserves his honor being in the Basketball Hall of Fame in Springfield, Mass. Meadowlark belongs with all the great, great, greats of our time in sports, but his No.1 love and passion is serving and living for the Lord in his life. Just for the record: If the world had more Meadowlark Lemons, it would be a much better place! I'm honored to call him my friend."

– Jimmy Walker, Founder of Muhammad Ali's Celebrity Fight Night,
friend, and Trustee of Harlem Globetrotters

♦

"Meadowlark Lemon is the definition of comedy basketball. He is an incredibly brilliant combination of a physical comedian who could hold an audience in the palm of his hand as well as have them in stitches with the things that he says and the timing with which he says them. He mixes the skills of the best Las Vegas magician's technique of close-up magic and the precision of the most graceful basketball player. There could be only ONE Meadowlark Lemon. I am honored to say that Meadowlark Lemon is my friend."

– Stuart Hersh, public relations professional, Hollywood promoter

♦

"Mercy Ministries has been blessed to call Meadowlark a friend. He has a way of connecting with people of all ages and backgrounds using his God-given sense of humor to not only make you laugh, but also to share the truth of God's Word in a unique way. Meadowlark never misses an opportunity to minister to our girls and we are so grateful for his heart for Mercy!"

– Nancy Alcorn, Founder and President, Mercy Ministries International

♦

"Meadow called and wanted me to guard Wilt Chamberlain on an NBC Sports World TV special. He was launching the Bucketeers at the time. I was to be on the 'stooge team' – the California Coasters. I went to training camp and was in intense sessions learning the tricks and the choreography of the show.

Meadowlark got this wild hair about being different. He called me into his office one day and asked me if I wanted to make 'sports history' by becoming the first white player to play comedy basketball alongside him, Wilt, Marques Haynes, Jumpin' Jackie Jackson, and many others. I asked him if I had to wear the Bucketeers' funky hats and he said I had to. I said 'OK' anyway.

After being an All-American basketball player, I was blessed to get the call from Meadow. It was amazing riding on that lemon yellow bus and looking at Meadowlark and the others who I had pictures of on my wall when I was growing up.

— Allen Winder, the "Blue-Eyed Soul Brother," Founder Adub Studios, and player for Meadowlark Lemon's Bucketeers

♦

"For people everywhere — whether a fan of basketball or not — you knew who Meadowlark Lemon was. I have fond memories of the antics Meadowlark performed on the basketball court and the happiness that emanated from him. He was not only an inspiration for what he achieved in the game, but is an inspiration for who he is as a person. It is an honor to know him."

— Fran Judkins, Senior Director of Professional Relations, Basketball Hall of Fame

♦

"Meadowlark, you are the best!"

— Jerry Colangelo, former owner of the Phoenix Suns and the Arizona Diamondbacks, CEO of the Basketball Hall of Fame

♦

"To my 1/2 brother, Meadowlark: May the Lord Jesus continue to open doors for you that no man can close! Thanks for your encouragement along the way!"

— Bob Wieland, "Mr. Inspiration," author of *One Step at a Time*, motivational speaker, and actor

♦

"I have been associated with famous people most of my life, but none more beloved than Meadowlark Lemon."

— Actor Bruce Locke (*Robocop 3, Mortal Kombat Conquest*)

♦

"I consider this a great honor and privilege to share about a good, trusting friend and co-worker, Meadowlark Lemon, #36. I told him the #3 stood for God and the #6 stood for man. When they're put together it stands for God-Man. Truly a remarkable ambassador of joy, I've seen people come into his presence and begin to laugh spontaneously!

It's unlikely that an outsider would be welcome in the trust of the people on the reservations. When he conducted a basketball clinic in Low Mountain, Ariz., the Indian children were thrilled to receive a Meadowlark Lemon basketball and T-shirt. It was there that I saw his amazing ability to work with the Navajo children with the same professional skills that he demonstrates in every area of his life. His dream is to motivate Native American athletes to reach professional status. That first clinic resulted in several invitations to Indian reservations. It was there that we introduced him to Fry Bread. When he conducted a clinic in Auburn, Calif., he joined the Indian children in the Indian friendship dance. We gave him the name "Chief." His countenance lit up and a big smile came across his face. It's an awesome feeling to get to work and play as a member of the Harlem All Stars, as well. He made me an official player. My instructions were to "just stand there until we give you the ball. Don't try to make the basket, and don't chase after the ball. We will get it." To everyone's amazement, I made six points. You will probably cry, laugh, and jump for joy as you read this man's life. God bless you, #36."

> – Pastor Ray and Ceci Ramos, friends and partners in our
> outreach to American Indians, Festival of Life World Outreach Ministries,
> The United Auburn Indian Community, Auburn, California

◆

"Meadowlark Lemon is a living basketball legend and a household name. In fact, his name is one of the most well known, not just in America, but in all the world.

The late, great basketball Hall of Famer Wilt Chamberlain described Meadowlark Lemon as the greatest basketball player he had ever played with or witnessed.

Meadowlark Lemon is much more than just a world-renowned basketball player. It's been my privilege to have been his friend and pastor for the past 18 years. I discovered Meadowlark to be one of the most humble, kindest and giving persons I've ever met. He has given of himself to countless charitable causes, churches and individuals. He has the heart of a servant and is constantly engaged in helping people. Meadowlark Lemon is not just a great athlete, he is a great person."

> – Pastor Michael Maiden, Church for the Nations, Phoenix, Arizona
> home church pastor to the Lemon family

◆

"Meadowlark is poetry in motion, coupled with charisma, charm, and character, captivating crowds around the world. He is a 'globe-trotter' in more ways than one. He is leadership and laughter intertwined and JOY could be his middle name. He is more than the Clown Prince of Basketball, he is a class act in the Game of Life.

Society suggests that 'good guys come in last.' Mr. Lemon reminds us that not only can good guys win in the end but they can laugh loud, enjoying the journey in the process.

Over the years I have met quite a few people, but no one with the heart, work ethic, and genuine love for others that Meadowlark has. He is more than a showman, he is a spokesman of truth that transcends race, time and culture.

His new book is more than a slam dunk, it will 'assist' you to score like never before in every aspect of life. 'The Greats are Gracious' and Meadowlark Lemon is both."

> – Frank Shelton, author, motivator & friend

◆

"Meadowlark brings a lifetime of wisdom and experience to life in this book. I love his stories and his straightforward, no-nonsense approach to life and living. He is a wonderful servant to his God and his fellow man. Meadowlark Lemon is a true National Treasure."

> – Todd Perry, CEO/Executive Director, The Pujols Family Foundation

TRUST YOUR NEXT
SHOT

A GUIDE TO A LIFE OF JOY

MEADOWLARK
LEMON
with Lee Stuart

ASCEND
BOOKS

www.ascendbooks.com

Requests for permission should be addressed Ascend Books, LLC,
Attn: Rights and Permissions Department,
10101 W. 87th Street, Suite 200, Overland Park, KS 66212.

10 9 8 7 6 5 4 3 2 1

Printed in the United States of America
ISBN-13: 978-0-9841130-4-0
ISBN-10: 0-9841130-4-5
Library of Congress Cataloging-in-Publications Data Available Upon Request

All photos courtesy of Meadowlark Lemon unless otherwise indicated.

Illustrations by Craig Lueck
Editors: Jon Rand and Cindy Ratcliff
Design: Lynette Ubel

www.ascendbooks.com

Dedication

To all the fans around the world and to our men and women in uniform who continue to make the United States of America a place of freedom where people can find joy and strive to live their dreams.

To the greatest team of all: my family. You are the most cherished gift that God has ever blessed me with and you bring me great *joy*.

Table of Contents

FIRST HALF – THE BALL GETS ROLLING

SECOND HALF – TRUST YOUR NEXT S.H.O.T.

I was blessed to be inducted into the Basketball Hall of Fame in 2003.

Acknowledgements

To my MVP and wife, Dr. Cynthia Lemon, for being my love, for taking great care of me, and working side by side with me for almost 20 years and sharing my vision to bring joy to the nations.

To all of my children, whom I love dearly, each one of you is a unique expression of my life. Thank you for your love, which brings me much joy, and for your patience and sacrifice as I traveled the world. You get the credit for all I do. Special thanks to my daughters, Crystal and Angela, for your untold hours of faithful service to our ministry and to this book.

Many thanks to Bob Snodgrass and Lee Stuart and our friends at Ascend Books. Your diligent work and tireless efforts have made a book we are proud of. We are thankful it is your organization we partnered with to bring the message of my life to the public. God bless you.

To the Harlem Globetrotters, who inspired me to dream about basketball as a young boy, who gave me the opportunity to wear the red, white, and blue, and who helped fulfill my dream of becoming part of the Harlem Globetrotters Team – the "Ambassadors of Good Will in Short Pants." We worked hard, and we had a lot of fun together trotting the globe. Thanks for the memories.

To my fans across the globe, I cherish the memories as much as you do. *Thank you.*

Introduction

Welcome to the world of Meadowlark Lemon – Basketball Hall of Famer and the renowned "Clown Prince of Basketball." The man with the most recognizable face and name in sports history!

Meadowlark's new book – *Trust Your Next Shot* – reaches beyond the 94' x 50' dimensions of a basketball court. It reveals the inner philosophy of the legendary Harlem Globetrotter who has dared to overcome poverty, racial prejudice, and scores of other roadblocks that surely would have sidelined most any other person.

Trust Your Next Shot reveals in clear, pointed language what has enabled Meadowlark to transform a rare combination of athletic prowess and side-splitting humor into a joyful formula for success that's sure to help you in business, in personal relationships, and in the demands of everyday life.

The book is funny, exciting, and refreshing – just like Meadowlark himself.

So join the man who helped change the face of American history, Black history, and sports history, the man who played basketball before kings, queens, presidents, popes, and maybe even you, as he teaches us all how to live a life of *joy!*

FIRST HALF
The Ball Gets Rolling

Let's throw the ball up and get this game started! This book is divided into two halves, just like a basketball game. These "halves" cover different periods of my life and the most important things that I've been involved with along the way. They are not chronological because, many times, things happen during one period of your life that you don't quite understand until later. Many situations that seemed like challenges at one time are revealed as blessings another time. What we thought of as small opportunities in our 20s turn out to have been some of the most important moments of our lives when we look back in our 50s.

Basketball games are played straight through from the first jump ball to the final buzzer. Life takes twists and turns. So, too, this book.

The First Half is about my growing-up years, my dream of becoming a Globetrotter, and the miraculous tryout I had with the team. It also covers many of the important people in my younger life, such as my dad, Meadow Lemon, Jr.; my volunteer coach, Poppa Jack; and, later on, Abe Saperstein, the owner of the Globetrotters.

It carries me right up to my "glory years" when I traveled the world with the most famous team there ever was.

The Second Half is about my beliefs and philosophies on how to get the most out of life and how to give and receive the most special gift of all – joy.

Before people wanted to "be like Mike," Mike wanted to be like me! People are always asking me everywhere I go, "How do you do that, Meadowlark? You always look the same!" I'm here to let you know that you have a choice every day about what you will or will not become. Not deciding is also a decision. I've had ups and downs in my life. I've never once lost faith or the desire to be everything I can be. When I tell you to "Trust Your Next Shot," well, I know what I'm talking about.

– Meadowlark Lemon

"*I will permit no man to narrow and degrade my soul by making me hate him.*"

– Booker T. Washington

Chapter 1

The Most Important Saturday of My Life

Wilmington, North Carolina

My life of joy began when I was 11 years old on a Saturday morning at the Ritz Theater in my hometown of Wilmington, North Carolina.

My friends and I would go to the Ritz every Saturday to watch movies from 10 o'clock in the morning until two minutes before 8 o'clock at night, which would give me just enough time to run home to meet my curfew of 8 o'clock sharp. For 25 cents, we could spend the whole day watching the westerns and the adventure movies that were so popular at that time.

Along with several feature films were three or four cartoons and a newsreel. A newsreel was a short film about an important or interesting story going on in the world. Remember, this was before television.

The newsreel on this particular Saturday was about a new kind of team – a basketball team known as the Harlem Globetrotters. The players in the newsreel were unlike any I had ever seen. We first saw them as they were in the locker room getting ready to go out on the court. I could hear them singing as they were lacing up their shoes. They were so happy just to be preparing to play a game.

When they ran onto the basketball court, wearing what the

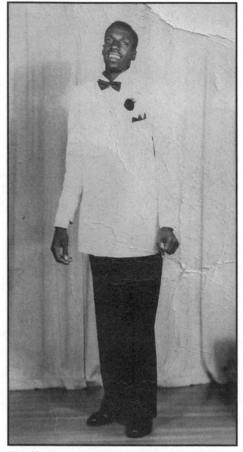

That's me, as a teenager, not too long before my tryout with the Globetrotters.

newsreel announcer described as bright red, white, and blue uniforms, I imagined vivid colors bursting off the black-and-white film. These incredible athletes seemed to make that basketball talk. They could make it sing! Their passes were crisp and clean. Their lay-ups looked like ballet. Their teamwork was amazing. They laughed, danced, and did ball tricks as they stood in a "Magic Circle" and passed the ball to a jazzy tune called "Sweet Georgia Brown." How they could play!

There was one other thing that was different about them, though. They were all black men. The same color as me.

I was mesmerized. At that very moment, something happened inside me. I knew beyond all doubt that I wanted to be a basketball player. For the first time, I was getting a vision of where my life was going to go. When I saw that newsreel, I saw it with *my heart, my soul, my spirit.* The other 300 people in that theater saw it only with their eyes.

That vision of my future didn't end with the newsreel. It followed me home that day, and it eventually became my life. Even though I didn't know it at the time, I had taken the first step toward becoming Meadowlark Lemon, the "Clown Prince of Basketball."

Before the Vision

Before I saw the newsreel that changed my life forever, I was like most of the other kids who grew up in Brooklyn, which was what we called the black section of Wilmington. We were born into a world of racism and segregation. Signs reading "Colored" and "White" separated public restrooms, drinking fountains, waiting rooms at the train station, and dining areas in restaurants. At the Bijou Theater downtown, white children would watch the Saturday morning movies from the main floor, and blacks were ushered upstairs to sit in the balcony. It wasn't easy growing up in a place and at a time when you were considered a second-class citizen just because of the color of your skin.

I had a few other challenges, too. My mom and dad divorced before I even started grade school. Divorce was very unusual in those days. My mother, who was a slender, beautiful woman, moved to New York City when I was about five years old to try to become a model. She got a few jobs for magazine ads. There was not a high demand for black models. She ended up cleaning hotel rooms to earn money. As I got a little older, I rode the train from Wilmington up to Harlem to spend the summers with her. I always had to return to North Carolina before school started again in the fall.

My father was Meadow Lemon Jr. He was a worker for the Wilmington Waste Paper and Recycling Company. My dad, who everyone called "Peanut," was tough. You didn't mess with him. He was known around town as a gambler's gambler. Some people said he made the bulk of his income from gambling in card games on the streets. He carried a switchblade knife, set halfway open with a piece of a match stick, so that the handle dangled outside his pocket. There was a local legend that my dad was so fast with that knife that he once snapped it open and had it at a man's throat during a card game before the man could even blink.

After my parents split up, I was sent to live with my Aunt Maggie and Uncle Frank and their seven kids. We lived in a tiny little house that also was the home to a couple of my dad's brothers and to their mother, my grandmother.

My dad lived about a block and a half west of us with his common-law wife. I saw him quite a bit and he kept close track of me. I even helped him with his job sometimes. When Aunt Maggie or my Grandma or one of the other seven kids made me mad, I would pack up everything I owned in a pillowcase and head up the street to spend a day or two with my dad.

That's my boyhood home in the Brooklyn section of Wilmington, N.C. I had an opportunity to return to my roots in August of 2010.

Even though people thought it was for the best that I didn't live with him permanently, I still idolized him.

I knew my dad loved me even though he wasn't big on saying "I love you." He proved he loved me more than life itself when an incident happened when I was four or five years old.

Dad and I were running to get across the street before traffic came to the intersection. Suddenly, I tripped and fell. I could not get up quickly enough to get out of harm's way. When my father saw this, he immediately turned around and threw himself on top of me as protection from an on-coming truck. It was his way of saying: "If anyone gets hurt it will be me, not my son."

Fortunately for both of us, the driver of the truck slammed on his brakes and stopped only a few inches short of us.

When my dad picked me up and dusted off my trousers, I knew that he must have loved me enough to place his life in jeopardy to save mine.

Today it reminds me of the biblical teaching: "Greater love has no man than this, that a man lay down his life for his friends." My father showed me he had that kind of love for me.

As I reflect back, I am grateful that Aunt Maggie and Uncle Frank took me into their home. It was a true act of kindness. Lord knows, they had plenty of other mouths to feed and people to care for. I must admit, I had a stronger tie with my parents. I cherished the times I spent with them.

One of the sadder days of my youth came when someone revealed to me that my mother had written to my father asking about the possibility of the two of them getting back together. I was told that a neighbor lady received the letter by mistake. After reading it, she thought my father would be making a mistake by considering the proposal, so she crumpled the letter into a ball and tossed it into the nearest wastebasket.

To this day, I wonder what might have happened to me had the two of them gotten together again and I had been raised in a relatively normal household.

While I was growing up, I got love and help from my grandmother, too. I also got a few switches and whippins. She was a tough lady. She wasn't one of those grandmas who spent all day baking cookies. She was the one who taught me never to steal and never to lie because if you will do either one of those things, then there is nothing you won't do. They open the door to all the rest.

It saddens me to say that I really raised myself. I had adults around who cared for me by making sure I had food, clothes, and a roof over my head. In reality though, I raised myself knowing I was not at the top of anyone's priority list. One good thing about this was that I had quite a bit of freedom. I could stay up late practicing basketball long after most households had gone to bed.

All of these things happened in my life before that enlightening Saturday in the Ritz Theater. These things would simply become only background for my vision, my dream, my incredible journey to becoming a Harlem Globetrotter.

DREAMS

CREATE THE WORLD YOU DREAM OF WITH EVERY CHOICE YOU MAKE

My dream became real after countless hours of practice.

Getting Started on My Vision

When that short newsreel ended, I leaped out of my seat and ran up the aisle of the Ritz Theater. My friends shouted after me, "Slim, where you goin', man? The feature's comin' on next!" An adult voice said, "Don't be runnin' in the theater, Meadow." I ignored them. I raced through the lobby of the theater, past the concession stand, and toward the door. "Hey! Slow down! If you leave, you can't get back in without payin'!"

It didn't bother me that I had just spent 25 precious cents on a few cartoons and a newsreel. I knew that what I had seen was somehow worth everything I owned.

I ran as fast as my skinny legs would carry me, straight to my dad's house. I had to tell him about the Harlem Globetrotters. I didn't even know where he was — at work, out gambling, or asleep in his house. I burst through the door of his house and started hollering for him. No one was around.

My mind was churning. I just had to learn how to play basketball, find out where the team was from in Harlem, and get goin' on my career!

I ran into my dad's kitchen and quickly rummaged through a cupboard. I found an onion sack with only a few onions left in it, so I dumped them out, tore the paper label away from the netting, and cut a hole in the bottom of the sack.

Then, I went to an upstairs closet and got a wire coat hanger, which I pulled apart on my way back downstairs.

I found a hammer and some nails, and took all of my materials across the street to a big tree next to the Robinson's house. I climbed up that tree, balanced on a limb, and fashioned that onion sack and coat hanger into a net and a rim. I nailed the whole mess to the trunk of the tree, maybe eight or nine feet off the ground, and climbed back down.

Now I had a basket. That was only half of what I needed to play basketball.

I went back to my dad's house, put the hammer back in its place, and looked around for something I could use as a ball. After several minutes of searching, I found an empty Carnation evaporated milk can in the garbage. It was the closest thing to being round that I could find!

I ran back to my homemade hoop and tried to remember how the Globetrotters in that newsreel had held the ball, how they had brought it up to shoot it. At first, I just threw the milk can like a baseball, and about every 10th "shot," it would drop through the net.

I shot and I shot that milk can until my dad got home. As soon as I saw him, I raced toward him. "Dad! Dad! I know what I want to be when I grow up! A Harlem Globetrotter! It's a basketball team! They are great! They sing and dance and play basketball and they have guys named Goose and Sweetwater and Rookie and I'm gonna be one!"

I asked him to watch me shoot. After several misses, I hit the net just so and the whole rim came tumbling down. I yelled across the street where he was watching: "Wait a minute!"

I scrambled up the tree and hung the rim again. By the time I got back down on the ground and had begun to shoot again, I noticed my dad had gone inside his house. I couldn't really blame him. I don't suppose it was much fun to watch me throw that can against a tree.

I stayed out there practicing until my friends came home from their day at the movies. We all tried to play this game that was new to us. One of my friends got the idea to try a tennis ball instead of the milk can. We also tried a softball for a while. Even though none of us were good, that didn't stop me from believing I was going to be a great basketball player one day.

I knew in my heart that I would practice, and work at it, and that I would give myself to this game until I was good enough to become a Globetrotter.

Even though that was a long time ago, I still believe to this day that God planted that dream in my heart as I sat right there in the Ritz Theater. He gave me a relentless desire, determination, energy, and the talent to make my dream come true.

I knew all great things come with a price and becoming a Globetrotter would take endurance and sacrifice as I focused on perfecting my game.

"I have always believed that if you put in the work, the results will come. I don't do things halfheartedly. Because I know if I do, then I can expect halfhearted results."

– Michael Jordan

Chapter 3

Poppa Jack and the Hook Shot Heard 'Round the World

Wilmington had an old, dilapidated USO building that had been made into a Boys' Club, and my friends and I would go there to hang out, horse around, and play different games. Of course, for me, the one and only game to play had become basketball.

At this time in my life, I was a skinny kid who was not blessed with much strength or impressive height. In order to compete on the basketball court, I had to learn to use skills that would allow me to have an advantage over taller, stronger opponents. One way to do that was to shoot so nobody could block the shot, no matter what size advantage he might have. The challenge was, how?

Enter a man named Earl "Poppa Jack" Jackson, and my life changed again.

Most of you have probably never heard of a man named Earl Jackson. That's because he never got the opportunity to showcase his talents on a big-time football field because of a severe knee injury he suffered during a practice session when he was a freshman at North Carolina State University. Surgery was unable to repair the damage, so he had to be content with being a spectator for the rest of his life.

Being a spectator, however, was not the kind of future that was acceptable to this special man. He focused his talents on becoming a coach, and believe me, he knew how to coach!

There was only one problem: With no college degree, Jackson was unable to land a position on the staff of a high school or college. So he took the next best option. He became a volunteer at the Boys' Club of Wilmington.

What Poppa Jack may have lacked in formal credentials, he made up for with good, old-fashioned intuition. He just had a feeling that a certain youngster had enough talent to rise above the average.

Some would call it a "sixth sense"; others might call it a "gut feeling." Whatever it was, he had it.

Poppa Jack picked me out of all the kids who were playing a pickup basketball game one afternoon at the Boys' Club.

"What's your name, son?" he asked me.

"Meadow, sir. Meadow Lemon," I said, trying to be polite and hiding the fact that I was intimidated by his size and gruff exterior.

"Well, Meadow Lemon, I have seen you play and you sure seem to love this game."

"Yes, sir. I sure do," I said.

"Let me tell you, son," he went on. "If you continue to play as you are doing, you might do OK. How would you like for me to show you a shot that, if you get it right, could make you unstoppable on the court?"

I listened intently, even though I was somewhat skeptical. He truly seemed to believe what he was saying.

When I didn't respond immediately, Poppa Jack drew himself up to his full 5'10" frame and asked sternly, "Well, do you want me to show you or not?"

"Ahhh, yes, sir," I said. "Yes, sir!"

He led me to a spot about 10 feet in front of one of the baskets. "OK," he said. "Stretch out your right hand as far as you can."

When I did, he placed the ball on my outstretched palm.

"Turn your back to the basket."

I did just that.

"Now toss the ball into the basket."

I turned to face the basket.

"Look, I didn't say for you to turn around," he ordered. "Look over your shoulder if you wish, then toss the ball over your head. Do not turn around."

Is he crazy? I thought. Even if I turn my head as far as it will go, I can barely see the rim of the basket.

"Go ahead," he said. "Don't be shy. Let the ball go."

I did. The ball went straight up toward the ceiling and hit nothing but air. It landed on the floor and rolled against a wall.

"That's OK," he said. "Go pick up the ball and do it again."

I did. I returned to the same spot and tried again.

Nothing but air.

"Keep practicing that shot," said Poppa Jack. "I'll be back tomorrow to see how you're doing."

I spent the rest of that afternoon throwing that hook shot toward the basket.

Occasionally, I heard the ball hit the rim of the basket with a dull THUNK! Most of the time, however, it just fell to the floor.

After a full hour, the THUNKS outnumbered the airballs. Mostly all I heard was: THUNK! THUNK! THUNK!

I had to get home for supper or I would get a lecture – or worse – from my grandmother who never tolerated me showing up late.

The next afternoon I was back in the gym, standing in exactly the same spot, shooting the same shot.

THUNK! THUNK! THUNK!

Suddenly, instead of a THUNK!, I heard a SWISH! The ball had actually gone into the net!

I leaped into the air in celebration as if I had just made the winning basket for the state championship.

"Nice going, kid," called the lone voice from the back of the gym.

It was Poppa Jack. He had been watching me for nearly an hour.

He walked over to me and gave me a few extra pointers, including how I should hold my left elbow high, level with my shoulder, and my left forearm at a right angle in order to ward off any opponent from getting close enough to block the shot.

"That'll give you another whole foot and will allow your ball to go higher without interference from a defender," he said.

I knew that I was being taught by the best coach I had ever known.

Poppa Jack gave me the ball and ordered me to practice the shot some more.

I did that whole afternoon.

And the next afternoon.

And the next.

Whenever Poppa Jack returned to the gym to watch me, he had me move a step or two farther from the basket.

I practiced that hook shot every day *for three full months.*

I was growing up, and I didn't even know it. The division between the races was becoming clearer to me, too. Just a few paces from my dad's house was a white elementary school, right in the center of the all-black Brooklyn area of Wilmington. I don't know if it had a gym, since we weren't allowed to enter. It had a huge playground though, enclosed by a brick wall and fence, which was also off limits. When the school day was over, we snuck in there, of course. Our softballs and footballs broke a few windows, and when a ball landed on the roof, we shimmied up the downspout. It's a wonder no one was killed on those rickety things. The police ran us out whenever they saw us on the playground, and that was frequently. As we got older, we got bolder, and we threw stones at the police cars just to get them to chase us. We knew it was wrong; however, we also felt it was wrong to run us off what we thought should have been a public playground right in our own neighborhood. It made us angry. We never tried to hurt anybody or anything, and we weren't quite brave enough to really risk getting caught. Being chased by the police was a little diversion in an otherwise tough existence. We suspected the cops enjoyed the activity, too. Often as we sat joking out on the brick wall, a squad car would pull by slowly, as if to warn us not to drop down the other side into the school yard. We always waited until dark, when the coast was clear, and someone had to stand guard. If he yelled that the cops were coming, we jumped the six-foot wall and ran between houses all over the neighborhood. The nearly nightly chase was almost as much fun as playing ball.

Following my three months of faithful practice, I got to the point where I was making the shot at least 10 percent of the time. Then Poppa Jack did something totally unexpected. He told me to stretch out my left arm. I did. "Now, do the same thing you've been doing with your right hand, only use your left."

I did, only this time without any questions.

After another six weeks, I could make this difficult hook shot with either hand.

That was the start of the shot that eventually would make me world famous.

Here's an important point: I did not stop practicing after I had perfected the shot. Throughout my entire professional career, I practiced that shot every day.

As I grew older and became a member of the Globetrotters, my percentage for making that shot increased to better than 70 percent from half court.

I practice that shot to this day as part of my daily workout.

As I said, I learned to perfect the hook shot because I was taught by the very best coach I've ever known.

No, it wasn't Poppa Jack.

It was me.

I eventually had to teach myself that hook shot. Poppa Jack showed me how to do it, and I had to make the decision to practice it, practice it again, and practice it even more. I could not depend on someone else to make the shot for me. I had to learn to do it myself.

Where can you find Poppa Jack today?

You can find him anywhere.

There is a "Poppa Jack" in every city and neighborhood in America and in the world. He goes by different names. You'll know who he is the minute you lay eyes on him.

He's the one who volunteers to coach young people at your local YMCA or Boys' and Girls' clubs, or out on the streets and sandlots.

He's the one not looking to have his name in the headlines or being honored at a banquet. He's the person whose sole mission is helping youngsters be all they can be.

There's one other thing: You won't need to look for him. He will find you.

"Keep your dreams alive. Understand to achieve anything requires faith and belief in yourself, vision, hard work, determination, and dedication. Remember all things are possible for those who believe."

– Gail Devers

Chapter 4

Gaining on My Dream

Let's fast-forward about 50,000 hook shots later ... to my days at Williston Industrial High School, the only black high school in Wilmington.

At Williston, which had about 400 students, I played three sports – baseball, football, and basketball – and sang bass in the glee club.

Well, saying that I played baseball might take a little explaining. My baseball "career" was pretty short.

During baseball tryouts my freshman year, the coaches were amazed by my natural defensive abilities. I really had a knack for getting to balls that had been hit into play. I caught everything that was hit or thrown my way, and batting seemed easy, too, mainly because the pitchers were my teammates and they were throwing easy pitches.

I didn't tell anyone that I was actually afraid of the ball! I had seen Larry Doby, the first black player in the American League, get beaned, and I didn't want any part of that. Plus, I knew that basketball was my main game, and I didn't want to risk my future in that sport by getting hurt in a sport that I didn't care about nearly as much.

Every day in practice I smashed line drives around the field, and learned to be a good base-runner. So the coaches put me into the starting line-up at first base for our first game.

My first inning in the field was like a movie nobody would believe. I had two putouts and an assist against the opposing team, and all three plays were far from routine: I snagged a hot line drive off the bat of the first hitter, stretched to the limits of my body to scoop a low throw from our third baseman against the second hitter, and made a nice play in shallow right field, snagging the ball and leading the pitcher covering first base with a perfect throw.

Now our team was up to bat. Our lead-off man, the best hitter on our team, struck out on three blazing fastballs from the opposing pitcher. Watching this, my anxiety began to build. I was scheduled to hit third in our line-up.

Our second batter took a white-streak fastball inside, which made me gasp in the on-deck circle, then struck out on three straight pitches.

So now it's my turn to stand in against this pitcher, who was a senior in high school and being scouted by major league teams.

I planted myself deep in the batter's box, so if he hit me with a pitch, it would have to be deliberate. His first pitch came in high and hard, and, having already made up my mind to swing as hard as I could three times and get it over with, I lunged at the ball.

My baseball "career" was brief! Here I am with some of my Army teammates. I was a good fielder, I just was afraid of the fast pitching!

The bat recoiled in my hands as I made contact with the pitch. Incredibly, I had hit the ball with the sweet spot of the bat, and it screamed toward the right-center field gap, rising as it went. The right fielder and center fielder just turned to watch it fly by. If there had been an outfield fence, it would have cleared it easily. As it was, the ball bounced and kept rolling. I sprinted around the bases, both scared and excited, and somewhere between second and third decided that baseball was not for me.

I was naturally good in the field with the glove. I was just afraid of the pitching. The home run had been luck. I might play a long time before I hit another, and I just couldn't see myself standing in against older, stronger pitchers.

So, when I got to our dugout, I accepted all the congratulations from my teammates and coaches, then told my coach, "I quit. I'm sorry. I'm done. The pitching is too fast for me."

He tried to talk me out of it – and my teammates gave me some ribbing – I stuck to my decision. My baseball "career" was over.

I am remembered for being a Hall of Fame basketball player; however, few people know that I was a very good football player in high school. Very good. All-State good. I was a receiver on offense and a cornerback on defense. I could tackle well, catch passes well – sometimes even with one hand – and I was a good blocker when a play called for me to do that.

As a freshman defensive back, I got torched by a great runner from another team – J.C. Caroline, who ended up playing in the National Football League for many years. He caught everything thrown his way, and I did little to slow him down. So after that wake-up call, I asked to take one of the school's tackling dummies home to practice with. The coaches agreed to let me borrow one, and I practiced on it constantly.

Eventually, I became an all-state athlete in both basketball and football. At 6'2" tall, I averaged about 30 points a game during my senior year of basketball. I made myself into an excellent football player, too. I got something like 70 college scholarship offers to play football and

60-some offers to play basketball. About 20 schools offered me a scholarship to do both.

Becoming all-state in basketball didn't happen without some struggles, however.

I played sparingly as a freshman. Although, because of an injury to our center, I did get into a game against Laurinburg Institute, a private school who had a pretty good player you may have heard of: Sam Jones, who went on to become a legendary guard for the Boston Celtics.

Playing against Sam Jones and Laurinburg's other bigger, better players made me realize that I wasn't quite ready for high-level basketball. I was a good neighborhood player. I understood the game's fundamentals and my natural talents and abilities were maturing. What I didn't really know much about were team concepts, proper defensive techniques, and all the other things you need to know to compete at a high level.

So I went to work, harder than ever. I was a madman in practice. If the coaches told us to run 10 laps around the basketball court, I would run 20. If they said shoot free throws until you sink 10 in a row, I would shoot until I had made 20 in a row. When my teammates called it a day and headed for the showers, I stayed on the court by myself and shot, dribbled, faked, and shot some more.

My hook shot was a good weapon, and I knew I still needed to develop an inside game, a man-to-man game, a zone game, a set of strong offensive skills, and a set of flypaper defensive skills.

If I was going to realize my dream of becoming a Globetrotter, I had to become a complete player. Nothing was going to stop me from reaching that goal. Not long hours of practice, not the pain of conditioning, nothing.

Not even a freshman English test.

Now that's an interesting story!

Mrs. Leonard, who we sometimes called "Mother" Leonard, was our English teacher at Williston. One day, after basketball season had ended my freshman year, some of the older guys introduced me to alcohol. Well, there is no other way to put it: I got drunk. Sick drunk.

I was out at a night club with some of my friends who were a few years older than I. One guy, Alan, kept after me to take a drink of Old Crow that he had in a brown paper bag. I told him no several times. "My dad would kill me if I drank that and so would my coaches."

Finally, he called me a chicken, and like a fool, I took a swig off that bottle. I wiped my lips with my hand and gave the bottle back to him.

"No, man. You got to say 'Ahhhhh,'" Alan said. "If you don't say 'Ahhhhh,' it don't do you no good."

I took the bottle again and this time I let seven or eight big swallows burn down the back of my throat. In a few seconds, the world started to spin. My eyes filled, my stomach churned, and my head buzzed. "Oh, man," I said. "I shouldn't have done that!"

Alan chuckled and said, "What you need is a chaser." I asked for water. He went off for a moment and brought back a frosty beer.

At this point, all I cared about was that my throat was on fire. I slugged down that icy cold beer, and for a while, my throat felt better. My stomach felt worse.

I stood up and began to stammer out some words that sounded kind of like "I gotta get home."

Alan steered me through the crowd of people in the club, out the door, and hailed a cab. He poured me into the cab's back seat, and the driver took one look at me and said, "Ain't you Peanut Lemon's boy?"

I nodded yes and he began to drive us to my dad's house. Along the way, he thought I was going to be sick in his car. We were about three blocks away from home. He pulled over to the side of the road and said, "Don't be throwin' up in my car, boy! You're getting out here and no charge. You can find your way from here, can't you, Meadow?"

I did. And let's just say I didn't have a real peaceful night.

I was supposed to take my freshman English final exam the next morning. I went to school with quite a hangover, and staggered into Mrs. Leonard's classroom. She took one look at me, left off what she was saying to the class, and marched me to the restroom. She helped me wash my face with cold water and told me to forget about the test, to go home and get some sleep.

For three years – all the way up through my senior year – I thought Mrs. Leonard had forgotten all about that freshman English final. Three days before I was supposed to graduate, she tracked me down and said, "Meadow Lemon, I don't care who you are or who you think you are or how big anybody else thinks you are. You will be takin' the freshman English final."

Oh, man. There was no way I could let a test stand between me and graduating. If I didn't pass it, I could be derailed on my path toward becoming a Globetrotter!

Mrs. Leonard gave me a little while to study for the exam, then put me in her class of freshmen to take the test. I bet I looked huge to those 14-year-olds. I was the big senior star athlete, all-state in two sports!

I got a 98 on that test. All because Mrs. Leonard insisted that I succeed.

I was gaining on my dream.

Chapter 5

The Dream Comes True:
My Tryout with the Globetrotters

The story of how I was given a chance to try out for the Harlem Globetrotters still seems like a dream to me, all these years later. Here's how it happened:

After I got the 98 on Mrs. Leonard's freshman English test and graduated from high school, I was hanging around Wilmington, waiting for the Globetrotters to discover me. This didn't make my dad any too happy. He wanted me to go to college so that I could have a chance at a better future. He coaxed me, grumbled at me, and even made me join him on his tough job with the waste paper company, lifting heavy cartons of paper into a truck. He reminded me that I had received all those college scholarship offers.

I didn't want to go play basketball or football at a college because I was afraid the Globetrotters might not be able to find me (when, I was sure, they would come looking for me).

One day late in the summer, I was passing the day away with friends, playing some baseball, some basketball, and some cards. My dad's truck pulled up to where we were sitting and he motioned me over. "Get in, Junior. It's time for school."

I asked, "What are you talkin' about?"

He nodded toward the back of his truck. That's where I saw my suitcases.

In my dad's shirt pocket was a train ticket to Tallahassee, Florida. A ticket to Florida Agricultural and Mechanical University (Florida A&M), where, in fact, I had been offered a dual scholarship to play both football and basketball.

I was not too keen on going to Florida A&M. I was frustrated that I simply couldn't will myself to be a Globetrotter. I was scared, too, of leaving home and entering the great unknown.

When I showed up for my first football practice at A&M, the coach told me there had been some mistake with my dual sports scholarship. "We don't give football-basketball combo scholarships anymore," he said. "The basketball coach thinks you pansies will get hurt out here."

So that was the sum total of my life as a football player in college. Not exactly Heisman Trophy stuff.

My scholarship for basketball was still good; all the paperwork for it was correctly in place. With it being only August, though, basketball season seemed years away.

When college classes started, I hadn't made many friends. I was too homesick. I wanted to get back on the train and leave Tallahassee behind.

I called home.

My dad and I chatted for a while on the phone, and I faked that I was doing OK at college. That's when he said: "I'll bet you're glad I sent you down there. Your draft notice came the other day. Since you're enrolled in college, you can get a deferral. I'll send all the paperwork to you and the school can help fill it out."

My mind turned upside down. I wasn't playing football ... basketball season was months away ... and all my dreaming hadn't yet gotten through to the Globetrotters.

So, I thought, I might as well join the Army, even though there was a war going on in Korea.

A couple of weeks later, I left Florida A&M and went back to Wilmington.

And back to a pretty upset Peanut Lemon.

Fortunately, one of my high school coaches, E.A. "Spike" Corbin, knew my dream was to play for the Globetrotters. He had written a letter to Abe Saperstein, the owner of the Globetrotters, and told him to keep an eye out for me after I finished high school.

He hadn't heard anything back yet. He did mention that the Globetrotters were touring through nearby Raleigh, North Carolina, in a few weeks. I coaxed Coach Corbin into calling Abe Saperstein to see if he could get us into the game. He called and actually got through to Abe! They talked for a few minutes, then Coach hung up and smiled.

"He says all we have to do is go down there and introduce ourselves to Marques Haynes. Abe won't be there. He said Haynes would get us in."

"*The* Marques Haynes?" I asked.

"Looks like it," Coach said. "And Abe said he would have Marques look you over. If you show him anything, he'll give you a shot."

"What does that mean?" I asked, wide-eyed.

"I don't really know. I'd take some trunks with you and be prepared to work out a little."

The Tryout

When the day of the Globetrotters' game in Raleigh finally arrived, Coach Corbin loaded me, Poppa Jack, and three of my friends into his car and we headed north.

The arena was overflowing with thousands of fans who had come to see the world-famous Harlem Globetrotters. We had a hard time finding Marques Haynes in the lobby because of the surging crowd. I finally spotted him, walking through the hundreds of fans who were reaching out to him, patting him on the back, and asking for autographs.

I said, "Mr. Haynes. I'm Meadow Lemon. Mr. Saperstein said we were supposed to ..."

He said, "You're Lemon? Yeah, Abe called me and said you'd be comin'. Let's go." He took me to the team's dressing room, then went to get tickets for my friends. When he came back, he told us that there weren't any tickets left. There wasn't even standing room available! So they would have to spend the game waiting around outside the arena.

In the dressing room, the legendary Goose Tatum introduced himself to me. He was putting on uniform Number 36 (which eventually became mine). After he got back from trying to find tickets for my friends, Marques introduced me to the team: Rookie Brown, Frank Washington, "Sweetwater" Clifton, and Clarence "Horse Cave" Wilson, who got his nickname from his home of Horse Cave, Kentucky.

I couldn't believe this was happening to me! My dreams and visions from the past came quickly to my mind. Here I was, a teenager just out of school, in the dressing room with my heroes! Could it get any better? Then, Marques handed me a uniform and told me to get dressed. "It's Showtime." My heart leapt in my chest!

I had seen the Globetrotters run onto the floor during the newsreel at the Ritz. Now I was running out with them! During team introductions, the announcer said:

"Ladies and Gentlemen, Boys and Girls, for the first time in a Globetrotter uniform, from Wilmington, North Carolina, Meadow Lemon!"

The arena shook with a sound I had never heard before or since.

While we were warming up in the lay-up line, I laid the ball against the backboard like I had been taught to do. Jumping Johnny Wilson said to me, "Let's show them how to dunk." Some of the other players shook their heads as if to say, "Yeah. Go ahead."

I was young and my legs were strong. I could really run and jump, so I said, "Let's do it!"

A few moments before the game was to get underway, Marques called the players together and told them, "No high-fiving or jumping up and down. Do your jobs."

All the players did their jobs – very well. At halftime, Marques told me that I was going into the game in the third quarter so the Globetrotters could see what I could do.

I said to myself, "You've got a tryout in front of 15,000 people or more! Make the most of it!" I played about a quarter-and-a-half and scored 12 points.

Everyone was happy with my play. A few of the players said, "Man, is he fast!" I just thought to myself: young legs!

I knew I had made a good impression. I thanked Marques for giving me the chance. I could feel that my dream was about to be fulfilled.

As I walked out of the arena after the game, I was signing autographs and felt like I was on Cloud Nine. My friends were waiting for me, as happy for me as I was for myself! The car ride back to Wilmington was a long one, and it was filled with joy!

"I don't care how slow or fast you are — or how far you have to go — one step at a time in that direction will eventually get you there."

– Marques Haynes

Chapter 6

The Dream on Hold

Based on my performance in the Globetrotters' game, there was no doubt I had taken a giant step toward achieving my dream.

Goose Tatum, the most masterful ball-handler there ever was, had told me after the game in the dressing room, "You're a good-lookin' ballplayer, Lemon. Did you enjoy it?"

Then he tried to persuade me that there was not much future in playing basketball and that I should go to college. I knew better. He and Marques were both making $15,000 a year, which was not too bad in the early 1950s.

After the game, Marques had told me, "You've got the fundamentals and the flash. The comedy will come with time. I'm gonna tell Abe just what you showed today. You take care now."

He said that if Abe liked his report of my play, I would get called to tryouts in Chicago at the end of the Globetrotters' season. I conveniently did not mention that I was about to go into the Army.

Being a Soldier

I didn't like the Army at first. They called it 16 weeks of basic training. It felt more like 16 weeks of hard labor! It got hot. I thought Fort Jackson, South Carolina, was the hottest place in the world.

There were times during my first days with the Army when I felt very lonely. I was just a kid without a place I could really call my own. I had really raised myself. Most people don't know that I changed my age so I could get into the Army.

I thought drill sergeants and officers were the meanest people on earth. Now I know they were just doing what they had to do to get us ready to serve in Korea if we were called.

Early one morning, we were going to Raleigh to be examined. The black soldiers were riding at the back of a bus. The racial unfairness saddened me. We had been sworn in together, blacks and whites, and we might be expected to give our lives for our country in battle, then when we stopped to eat, we had to go to separate areas.

There had been a public outcry about the number of black soldiers being killed in Korea, so the Army cut back on the number they sent over. That was good news for me; however, it didn't erase the underlying fact that the Army was prejudiced. A lot of black soldiers from my unit in Fort Jackson were among the first to die in Korea. I sometimes wonder whether delaying my induction a few weeks by going to Florida A&M saved my life.

As I was learning to fire a military rifle and doing all the other things a young solider does in basic training, my daily routine was interrupted by a telegram from home.

"DEEPLY REGRET TO INFORM YOU OF YOUR FATHER'S
UNTIMELY PASSING DUE TO ACCIDENTAL KNIFE WOUND.
RETURN HOME SOONEST."

I immediately called home and learned that the "accidental" wound had been inflicted by my dad's common-law wife. My world caved in. I had no home. I was alone. And I hadn't heard a thing from the Harlem Globetrotters. Within the hour I was on a bus for the eight-hour ride to Wilmington. I felt like I was walking through a fog. I barely noticed the sea of white faces in the front half of the bus or the black faces at the back. When I reached the back of the bus there were no seats available. Four were open in the front. Four seats that I could not sit in. I had to stand in the back of the bus until a black passenger got off. Sadness, grief, rage, and frustration were screaming inside me. Here I was, an all-state high school athlete, probably one of the youngest ever to play with the Globetrotters, I had received more than a hundred college scholarship offers in two sports, and was serving my country in the military. Now my father had been murdered, and on my trip home from the Army, I had to stand, let alone sit, in the back of the bus. I wanted to sob, and I didn't want anyone to notice. I buried my face in my shoulder. That way I looked like I was staring out the window. I was on my own, at 18 years old, and the tears wouldn't stop.

At that moment, I had doubts that my dream would ever come true. We've all been there. We have all had our deepest pain. It's times like these that your vision for the future carries you through the dark times to the next steps.

Chapter 7

If You Dream It, It Will Come

My dad's death left a big hole in my life. The Army doesn't wait long for you to grieve. You gotta get back to being a soldier. So, after attending his funeral and putting a few things in order, I returned to my duty.

After I got back into the rhythm of a soldier's day, I discovered that the training and drills weren't enough to distract me from my anger over my father's death and from my disappointment that I had not yet heard from the Globetrotters.

So I began to play basketball during our free time on the post. It wasn't much of a challenge for me. I dominated against other guys who weren't especially good athletes, and my anger and disappointment fueled me not just to win, but to make a statement: "I am a Globetrotter. I don't belong here. I belong with the greatest basketball team in the world."

Finally, my permanent military assignment came. I was to be stationed at Camp Roder in Salzburg, Austria. This turned out to be a stroke of good fortune. The general at Camp Roder was a basketball fan and he wanted to field the best sports teams in the Army. Word got around that I was looking to join the Globetrotters. Even though the general was skeptical, he agreed to give me a chance on the basketball team.

Let's just say I made the most of that chance. After our team's first 13 games, we had nine wins and four losses. I was averaging 55 points per game while the rest of the team averaged a total of 13.

In the games we lost, I was so tired I was held to 40 points or fewer. One night as we walked to the court I heard an opposing player say, "Let Lemon get his 40 and we can win this."

I took that as a direct challenge. I scored 75 points in the first three quarters of the game, and we led, 83-81, going into the fourth. I was so exhausted that I suggested we play a slow-down game the rest of the way. It worked. We won by one point. I wound up with 80 points.

One of my favorite memories of those games in Austria had to do with me showing off for the general. A point came in one game when I had a wide open, uncontested path to the hoop. I held the basketball in my right hand, jumped as high and as far as I could, and slammed the ball through the rim. The crowd was screaming – especially the general, who pumped his fists into the air and accidentally swung his arm and clobbered his wife, who was seated next to him.

She went sprawling while several enlisted men rushed to her aid. No one ever forgot the dunk that knocked over the general's wife!

Basketball was a great diversion as my military service ground on. Then, one day out of the blue, a very special letter arrived for me.

It was *the* letter – the one I had been waiting for since that magical night in Raleigh.

It said:

Dear Private Lemon,

I'm sorry that it has taken so long to get back to you. I received an excellent report on your game in Raleigh from our former coach Marques Haynes. You may have heard that he has left us to form a similar team. Congratulations on your great game and for being such an outstanding player. We will be playing in Vienna next month. If it would be convenient for you to get there, I would enjoy meeting you. A brochure is enclosed, telling exactly where and when we will be there. Hope you can make it, but I will understand either way.

Cordially,
Abe Saperstein
Harlem Globetrotters, Inc.

P.S. I was saddened to hear of the passing of your father.

Well, you can rest assured that I got the general's permission to go to Vienna, and I played so well that Abe offered me a contract with the Globetrotters for a 40-game tour they would be having in Europe the following year.

The dream was no longer just a dream. It was reality. I was a Globetrotter, just as I had known I would be since the day I ran out of the Ritz Theater!

Let's Talk About Dreams ... and Visions

Gail Devers, who was quoted earlier was known as the "fastest woman in the world." She overcame a thyroid disorder known as Graves disease that sidelined her in 1989-90 and nearly resulted in having both feet amputated. She went on to become a three time Olympic Gold Medalist and the first American woman ever to win the gold metal 3 times. She had a dream.

Every one of us loves to dream. Many of us work hard to make our dreams come true. Other dreams never quite materialize no matter how hard we work.

So instead of just dreaming about something and wishing for it to come true, I encourage you to get into the habit of creating *visions*.

Visions have been instrumental throughout my life. I truly believe that I would never have become the success I've become were it not for my visions.

I'm not saying that I can gaze into a crystal ball and predict the winner of next year's Super Bowl. However, I *am* someone who firmly believes that if I can visualize doing something before it actually happens, my chances of achieving that goal are even greater.

When I was 11 years old, for example, and I saw the newsreel featuring the Globetrotters, I was witnessing for the first time in my life the great game of basketball. I was also experiencing something else. I actually envisioned myself playing the game with those same players when I became older.

Can you believe that? Even though I had never before seen a game of basketball, I could see myself playing with those guys on the screen.

The alarming fact is that of the 300 or so young people who were in the same theater with me that morning and watching the same feature, I was the only one who was inspired to change my life because of it.

Why is that?

Why would I be the only one to race home with an entirely different outlook on life?

Why would I go to the effort to assemble a crude basketball hoop, nail it to a tree, and create a "ball" out of a Carnation milk can?

Why would I spend hours each day tossing that can into the hoop?

The answer is simple: While I was sitting in the theater and watching the Globetrotters, I didn't just look at a game. I actually saw myself putting on a uniform and playing with the likes of Reece "Goose" Tatum, Marques Haynes, and Nathaniel "Sweetwater" Clifton when I grew older.

That vision was what I consider to be my start on the road to success in basketball.

This approach to success in life is not unique to me. Others probably have this same formula for success – visualize yourself already achieving something, chart your course to success, then put your plan into action.

I do the same thing when I play a round of golf for any of the charity tournaments at which I appear each year. If I stand at the tee on a par-three hole and say to myself, "I don't think I can do this," my chances of making a good shot are pretty poor.

If I say, "I think I have a strong possibility of reaching the green," my potential for a nice shot increases.

When I stand at the tee, focus on the flag waving above the hole about 220 yards away, and actually visualize the ball leaving the tee upon the impact of my swing, sailing though the air, then landing next to the hole, my chances of making par, or even a birdie, loom larger.

I used this same approach when I played basketball.

Spectators would rise to their feet whenever they saw me, standing at center court, tossing a hook shot over my head into a waiting basket.

The records will show that toward the end of my career I made that so-called "impossible shot" more than 70 percent of the time.

Would you like to learn my secret for success? Here it is: Before I took the shot, even while facing away from the net, I actually visualized the ball leaving my hand and going through the hoop.

Years ago, we were playing in southern California. I had been making shots from everywhere. I guess the people thought, "I wonder what he is going to do next" because the arena got very quiet. I was standing on the free throw line at the opposite end of the court. It doesn't make any difference which free throw line it is, free throw means *free*. I didn't think I could miss. I shot the ball and it looked as if the ball stayed up there forever. I am happy we were inside – if we had been outside, that ball would have hit the clouds and somebody would have gotten wet. It hit nothing but net. The promoter met me at half time and said, "Teach me to do that hook shot." I said to him, "You saw it from the outside. That shot came from the inside out – from my spirit."

That same approach applies to other areas of life. True visions have transformed my time on this earth from mere existence to joyful living. As the saying goes, if you aim at nothing, you are sure to hit it.

A worthwhile life begins with a bold vision.

Can Your Vision Change?

The answer to that question is both yes and no.

If you have a proper vision, your basic concept remains unchanged. As you mature and circumstances become different, that vision often grows sharper and becomes more relevant to the needs of the real world.

I continue to think back to that Saturday morning in that movie theater when I first had the vision of playing for the Harlem Globetrotters. That vision became more defined as I not only made the team, I also developed into the team leader and the "Clown Prince of Basketball."

How can you create your own vision?

If you're going to be successful in your life, I believe that the picture you have of yourself fulfilling your dreams must have the following characteristics:

Your Vision Must Be Self-Developed

It is not something imposed on you by someone else. It must come from within. You cannot allow anyone else to impose his or her vision of life onto you.

I've seen many sons of famous athletes remain frustrated in life because they were unable to duplicate the talents of their fathers. One of the reasons for this lack of stellar success is that outsiders may have visualized the actions of their fathers. The sons never adopted these visions as their own.

Your Vision Must Be True to Your Nature

Not everyone is blessed with the same talents. If, for example, you stand 5' 6", you would be an unlikely candidate for the next opening as a center for the Boston Celtics. That does not mean, however, that you cannot pursue a vision that allows you to pursue your passion, even if it involves basketball.

The first owner and coach of the Harlem Globetrotters – Abe Saperstein – was only 5' 2" and became the shortest member ever elected to the Basketball Hall of Fame.

Your vision should involve something in which you are truly interested. It should capture something inside of you that's so gripping that you never lose that "morning eagerness" to be at work.

Your Vision Must Be Clear and Compelling

Let there be no question on the part of you or anyone else as to where you're going and how you're going to get there.

That vision inside of me continued to burn as I tossed that milk can into that makeshift hoop.

You may be working diligently at a job, and that's certainly important. Of even more importance, however, is your vision.

Some of you may think that your job has no rewards. Perhaps the only rewards are a paycheck and an annual vacation. If so, I challenge you to expand your vision.

Create for yourself more meaning in your daily 9-to-5 job.

See yourself as already being part of a bigger picture.

Some of you right now might say to yourself, "I don't have the ability. I'm too old to change. I don't have all the necessary equipment to succeed."

Not so. If I can start a career in professional basketball with an old coat hanger, an onion sack, and a Carnation milk can, think of all you can do with the endless possibilities before you.

The Law of Attraction

We hear a lot about the "law of attraction" these days. It works like the law of gravity. What you sow, you reap. What you put out comes back. It is all controlled by your own brain. You can choose to dwell on negative thoughts or you can choose to think about positive things that make you happy. Your brain puts out frequencies and the law of attraction dictates that, by magnetic pull, it has to bring that exact same frequency back to you. You need to learn how to put out the frequency of what you want. Your brain is the transmitter and receiver. Your thoughts are powerful – both positive and negative. We can control what we think about. The "how" doesn't matter. Just stay focused.

Every negative experience that comes into your life will help you clarify what you do want. Say, "I know I don't want this. Now, what *do* I want?"

Focus on what you do want. Talk about and think about what you do want.

How do you stop negative thoughts? Start counting out loud. When you speak out loud, your mind will automatically stop the negative thoughts. You will be thinking about what you are saying. How do actors change their emotions to act? They choose something to think about that brings on the emotion. If they are needing to "act" happy, actors will think of a time when they were really happy or what might make them happy if it happened. The same goes for "acting" sad. The actors may need to think of someone they loved dying or something else profoundly sad. The point is, the actor controls his emotions by making a choice.

When your attitude is right, you can have, be, or do anything you want. If you think you can, you can. If you think you can't, you can't. Either way, you're right.

If you have a big success, other people may say it was luck or a coincidence or maybe even a miracle! In reality, it's the law of attraction at work.

In life, 99.9% of success is what you think. If you continue to think what you've always thought, you will continue to get what you've always got.

Here's a great example of what we're talking about with vision. My friend from my high school team, Robert "Iron Man" Brooks, always knew our team would win. When we went to different towns to play basketball, he would say, "We already won the game. We just came here to get the score!"

And finally, when it comes to dreams, visions, and the power of our minds, remember: With God, all things are possible.

"No matter what your heartache may be, laughing helps you forget it for a few seconds."

– Red Skelton

Chapter 8

It's All in the Timing

One of my greatest assets is timing.

Timing, of course, is essential for comedians. I loved looking into the stands and seeing Dean Martin, Jerry Lewis, Bob Hope, Jonny Carson, Bill Cosby and all those guys. To me, these veterans of show business were masters of timing and were able to utilize that skill to draw laughs from millions of people throughout the years. Great timing is also necessary for athletes.

The Picture Frame Image

Earlier, we discussed visions and how important it is for me and for other athletes to actually see ourselves doing something before we attempt to do it.

I've known athletes who go one step further. They break down their maneuvers as if watching a slow-motion film, with the frames crawling by one at a time.

The good athlete can visualize his motions four or five frames ahead of what he's doing. That could be while driving for a basket, shagging a fly ball, or rushing toward the end zone for a touchdown.

The great athlete will look ahead 20 frames.

The superstar, on the other hand, looks ahead to infinity.

That kind of vision separates the average player from the one who gets star billing.

Is this kind of vision taught or is it something with which you are born?

It's both.

You must have some God-given talent in order to perform at a high level in any sport or activity. Then, when you practice enough – practice perfectly – it becomes second nature.

One of my favorite "reems" (tricks) was my "injury act." It developed into a major crowd pleaser. It all began with me dropping to the floor "in pain" after just the slightest contact with an opponent. It could have been my leg or my arm; all the audience knew was that I was hurt. When Wilt Chamberlain was on the team, he'd seize me like a rag doll and cart me off the court, with the ball still in my hand. By the time I

Abe Saperstein and future Baseball Hall of Famer Ernie Banks joined me at a fund-raising event.

would step up to the free throw line, everyone was in for a real surprise – especially the referee. When I shot the ball, it would soar upward, then snap back like a boomerang. I would try to get rid of the ball by tossing it at the referee, somehow, it snapped right back. When the referee told me to get rid of the ball, I'd pass him one that couldn't even move, it just wobbled around. Or he might get one that would deflate in his hands as soon as he caught it. It was amazing! You never knew what was going to happen when I stepped up to the free throw line. The audiences always loved being in on the joke and it was the timing and execution that made it perfect every time. Nobody loved the gags more than I did.

Timing Is Dynamic

The game of basketball is constantly changing.

Our founder, owner, and first coach, Abe Saperstein, made history. He enjoyed a lot of success when he introduced an all-black basketball team during an era in which black athletes were held back by the color line. It may surprise you to learn that when I first joined the Globetrotters, the entire National Basketball Association had only a handful of black players. Today, black players dominate the NBA.

Mr. Saperstein changed history with his timing! He sensed that the country was ready for the Globetrotters' brand of basketball and entertainment. He showcased some of the best basketball talent in the universe at that time. Looking at today's NBA stars, I can see the creative influence and inspiration of our team in this generation. The door is wide open for athletic excellence today. You are no longer judged by the color of your skin; you are judged by the command of your athletic

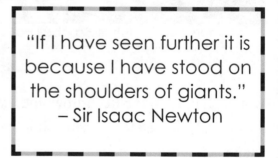

"If I have seen further it is because I have stood on the shoulders of giants."
– Sir Isaac Newton

presence. Abe Saperstein had great timing. I am looking forward to the day when I see every nationality represented in professional sports.

Let me tell you about the most important piece of timing that ever took place in my life. It involves a particular Saturday morning in a particular place and a particular show.

Remember the young Meadow being in the Ritz Theater on that Saturday in Wilmington, on the day he just happened to see that newsreel of the Globetrotters?

What if I hadn't been there for some reason? What if I didn't have the 25 cents to go to the movies that week? What if I had been sick or was away visiting my mother in New York?

It simply could not have happened. I believe I was destined to be there and see that film. If I hadn't had the money, I'm telling you, I would have found it on the street. Or someone would have come up to me with 25 cents and said, "Did you drop this money?" I was going to be there to see that film. No ifs, ands, or buts about it.

God wanted me in that theater seat to see the movie about those men making that basketball sing. He was in control of the timing. He knew it was time to set me on my life's mission.

I had faith even before I had faith. As I look back on my life, I realize that God was with me all the time.

"For I know the plans I have for you," declares the Lord, "plans to prosper you and not to harm you, plans to give you hope and a future."

– Jeremiah 29:11

Meeting the Man Who Changed My Life

Several men have helped change my life. Even though I didn't live with my dad when I was growing up, we spent enough time together for him to have a big effect on me. Earl "Poppa Jack" Jackson taught me the hook shot and encouraged me to be all I could be as a player and as a person. Coach Corbin was a blessing to me during my high school years. He said to me as I was leaving high school, "Well, kiddo, I've taught you all I know. Never cheat a friend." I have always remembered that wisdom.

Marques Haynes, Goose Tatum, and some of the other Globetrotters gave me encouragement during my incredible tryout with the team in Raleigh. I will always honor Mr. Abe Saperstein for giving me my ultimate opportunity to become a member of the Harlem Globetrotters.

Various drill sergeants and officers changed my life in the Army, even though I might not have liked what they had to say or what they made me do.

Of all the men I mentioned who helped make me into me, one man exists above all the rest: a man named Jesus Christ.

Those who know me today are aware that I am an outspoken non-denominational Christian evangelist. I am what you might call an independent preacher of the Gospel, the Good News, for any group that invites me to speak.

I have been invited to address both mainline churches and independent congregations. I've also appeared at less traditional venues such as prisons and shelters for the homeless. We minister to Native Americans, youth gang members, and those struggling with addictions in their lives. We do a lot of motivational and inspirational events where we team with other ministries and foundations and celebrity fundraisers for charities. We do large venues and small. We go to detention centers and lock up facilities and to youth prisons. We are looking at ways to focus on Native Americans in partnering with Pastors Ray and Ceci Ramos from California. (More on that later.)

In every one of these settings, the primary emphasis of my message remains the same: I come to you with a "Ministry of Joy."

It was a Jewish costume designer from Hollywood, California who introduced me to Jesus Christ, the man who has changed my life forever.

Here I am, proudly sporting the Bucketeers' uniform.

Here's the unlikely story.

After my playing days with the Globetrotters, I started my own comedy basketball team: Meadowlark Lemon's Bucketeers. As we were getting the team started, an agent helped us book several engagements, including a special on NBC's "Sportsworld."

This was great news. It would mean national exposure for our team, a chance to really show people what we could do!

There was one problem. We didn't have any uniforms to wear. I was given the name of a young costume designer who worked out of her home in Hollywood: Heidi Rasnow.

I consulted with her, told her about our deadline for the NBC show, and asked her if she would be willing to help with our uniforms. She agreed, and in a matter of days performed miracles with her sewing machine. She created magnificent uniforms, which was particularly difficult because she didn't have the measurements for most of the players! That included one HUGE set of measurements: for 7'1", 275-pound Wilt "The Stilt" Chamberlain!

She made the uniforms and they turned out great! We wore them on the David Letterman show and a young Dave told us he loved the uniforms. You can still watch the video clip of that appearance on YouTube.

During this time, I returned from a long trip with the Bucketeers and I felt compelled to stop by Heidi's studio when I got back. She was at the studio with a minister friend of hers, named John, who had also stopped by just before I arrived.

When Heidi saw me, she could tell that I had a lot on my mind. I had filled my life with everything that I thought would make a man happy: things, money, fame, security, work, busy-ness. Still, I wasn't happy. I was frustrated, disillusioned.

In her direct way, she said, "Meadowlark, I know what you need. You need Jesus." She knew it, and at that moment, I realized it, too. God had sent John to the studio at the same time God led me to go to the studio because God knew I needed him. "I'm ready," I whispered.

John led us in a simple prayer: "Heavenly Father, I come to you in the name of Jesus Christ. Your Word says whoever shall call on the name of the Lord shall be saved. I'm calling on you. I pray and ask Jesus Christ to come into my heart and be Lord of my life. I confess that Jesus Christ is Lord and I believe in my heart that God raised him from the dead. Thank you that your spirit now lives in me and I am forgiven. Amen."

After saying the prayer, I wish I could say my life changed completely in the next instant. There were no flashing lights and sirens as I would have expected. I was sincere when I prayed. I really did want the Lord's presence in my life. In the coming weeks and months my faith grew. I realized that God had cleaned me up on the inside and my desires had changed. I wanted to know more about the Lord and His word and I wanted to learn anything I could about having a closer relationship with the Lord. In less than a year, I began sharing my testimony about the prayer that changed my life. As I began to realize *who* I *was* and *whose* I was, I saw that God had known me even when I didn't know Him. God had been with me all the time. I read in the Bible that God gives us the desires of our hearts. When I read that, I realized when I went into the Ritz Theater at 11 years old that God was there, too. He gave me the gift of seeing a glimpse of my future with the Globetrotters on that movie screen. It must have delighted God when He saw me get so excited and run out of that movie theater to make my own basket. God was there when I was frustrated that I had no place to play and God gave me the courage to keep on believing that a little black boy going from home to home, no place to call my own, would have a chance to be on a team known around the world – the Harlem Globetrotters. God was there all the time guiding me, comforting me and encouraging me. He was with me when I thought I was alone, practicing for hours while my buddies were off doing other things. God was there all the time waiting patiently for me to recognize His presence in my life and go running into His arms! What a wonderful place to be: in the arms of God who brings unspeakable Joy. I knew, with all my heart, that Jesus Christ was the man who changed my life *forever.*

Anyone can say the prayer that John taught me and God will change their life the same way He changed mine. After saying it, I was assured of God's love and of eternal life, no matter what. If you're uncomfortable with this prayer and you're not sure about God, I challenge you just to pray:

"God, if you are real, reveal yourself to me."

You will be amazed at how God will make Himself known to you.

When I was a youngster, I used to sleep with a basketball. Now, whenever I get a hotel room while I'm traveling, the first thing I do is unpack my Bible and my study notes and put them on my bed. I study God's word in the same way I studied my basketball game.

A Once-and-Forever Globetrotter

We've entered an incredible period of my life – the more than two decades I spent with the world-famous Harlem Globetrotters.

We'll talk about my years as a player. This time of my life is loaded with memories and stuffed with lessons about racial equality, the power of fame, and the opportunities that came to me because I could shoot a ball into a basket.

Young kids used to say to me, "Hey, Meadowlark, it must be great to play for a team like the Harlem Globetrotters." They were right. I had the best of times, traveling the world, making children of all ages shout with laughter and excitement. Our audiences included popes, kings, queens, movie stars and maybe even you!

With the Globetrotters, God blessed me with a wonderful opportunity and the skills to make the most of it.

I call myself a "once and forever Globetrotter."

"The Globetrotters meant more to the NBA than the NBA meant to the Globetrotters."

– Frank Deford, renowned sports journalist

Chapter 10

Being Part of a Bigger Story

It's likely that no one ever would have heard of me if it hadn't been for the Globetrotters. I guess I could have made a name for myself as a football player at Florida A&M, or maybe I could have caught on with another basketball team. The Globetrotters helped make me as much as I helped make them. I like to think of myself as being a part of a much bigger story: the story of how the Globetrotters changed how black athletes – how all black people – were seen in America and around the world.

The Globetrotters were never from Harlem, you know. They were from the South Side of Chicago. They were made up of players who had played at Wendell Phillips High School, with the Giles Post American Legion team, and from a semi-pro team called the Chicago Ballroom Big Five, named after the famous Savoy Ballroom in Chicago.

The famed team was originally known as Tommy Brookins' Globe Trotters, and they wanted to take their game outside of Chicago and tour through the Midwest. Brookins was a black man and he knew it would be hard for him to book games against white teams in states like Michigan and Wisconsin. So by 1927 he had hired a young Jewish guy named Abe Saperstein to promote the team. Abe's family had come to the United States from England when he was a child. His father was a tailor, and, seeking a better life, moved his wife and 10 children from London to Chicago in 1906. Abe played basketball and ran track in high school, and attended one year of college before his money ran out.

So, when the opportunity to manage Brookins' team came along, he jumped at it.

It didn't take long for Abe to take over the team and give it a new name: the Harlem Globetrotters. In those days, the word "Harlem" was like a big billboard that shouted "This is a team of black players."

Someone asked him about the Globetrotters part of the name. He said he wanted people to think the team had been around the world. In a moment of truth he said, "I really just want to be able to play games outside the state of Illinois!"

In those early years, the Globetrotters would barnstorm through small towns and take on town teams from the local businesses, or college kids from the local area, making perhaps $75 for a night's work. The games always matched whites against the traveling black players. The Globetrotters not only whipped all their opponents, they also made fools of them in the process.

The scores got to be so lopsided that the Globetrotters began to do fancy passing drills and ball tricks to kill some time. That got laughs, and it also had the effect of holding down the score to make it more likely they'd get invited back the next year.

One of the biggest moments for the Globetrotters happened in 1948 when they went up against the Minneapolis Lakers, the best team in the NBA. The Lakers had the best big man in the game at that time, 6'10" George Mikan. The Globetrotters played them straight-up and beat the Lakers, 61-59, on a last-second shot. More than 17,000 people saw that game at Chicago Stadium.

That win was called a fluke by a lot of people who just couldn't believe that a bunch of black players could beat the best white team around. So, to prove it was no accident, the Globetrotters beat the Lakers again the next year, 49-45, and even clowned around some for good measure.

In 1951, the Globetrotters were used by the U.S. State Department as ambassadors of goodwill early in the Cold War. The Communist Party was putting on a big festival in Berlin, Germany, and two million people were supposed to be there. So, as a show of America's presence, the

United States arranged for a game in Berlin's Olympic Stadium. Keep in mind, this was only six years after World War II was over. The stadium had not been damaged by bombing during the war, so the State Department flew in three huge airlift planes with the Globetrotters, their opponents, the Boston Whirlwinds, a portable basketball court, baskets, and all the other necessary equipment.

Another important black athlete was part of that show: Jesse Owens. Jesse had won four gold medals at the Olympics in Berlin in 1936. And you might remember that the Nazi dictator, Adolph Hitler, would not shake Jesse's hand. It seems Jesse had put a pretty good dent in Hitler's philosophy that black people, just like Jews, were inferior.

Well, at halftime of the Globetrotters' basketball game, a helicopter comes over the stadium and lands in the middle of the field and out steps Jesse Owens. He was wearing a fine suit as he waved to the crowd. Then he kind of disappeared behind a group of Globetrotters for a few minutes, then popped out wearing his track suit! He took a lap around the stadium and the crowd noise was deafening.

This marked another breakthrough moment for black people.

These events were before my time with the Globetrotters. I wanted to remind you of them because I knew when I joined the team that they were one of the most important institutions in the world. They had done more for the perception of black people and for the perception of America than almost anything else you could think of.

I had played with the Globetrotters on a 30-day, 40-game tour of Europe while on leave from the Army. I was discharged from military service in December 1954, and played with the Globetrotters at a short training camp in February 1955.

Some of the best athletes and basketball players in the world were at that camp. There were about 125 guys competing for four or five full-time roster spots. Most of the players could fly, shoot the ball like a rocket, and run like a wild deer eluding a hunter. I didn't know what I had gotten myself into.

Every day we pushed ourselves to the limit. I remember going back to my hotel room, locking the door, pulling the blinds, turning off the lights, and praying to God I'd make it another day.

I had to make the team because I didn't have any real alternatives: my dad was dead, my mom was settled into her life in New York, my grandmother and Aunt Maggie had moved far away from Wilmington. I was, for all practical purposes, homeless. I had nowhere to go.

So Carl Green, one of the other players at the camp with whom I stay in touch to this very day, offered these words of wisdom: "Meadowlark, we got to ball!"

And ball we did.

I made the team, except it was not the one I was expecting. The organization assigned me to the Kansas City All-Stars. They were one of the Globetrotters' touring opponents. I played with them for two weeks, then was assigned to the Globetrotters' Southern unit. The main touring team, the Eastern unit, would be in Europe until mid-April, then I would have an opportunity to begin my journey to becoming one of the all-time greats of the Globetrotters.

Midway through my first full season, I was called up to the main Eastern unit to replace a player who was temporarily unavailable. Mr. Saperstein told me he wanted me to take over as the lead comedian. From somewhere deep within me came a joy and even a voice that I can only use while I'm on the court in the heat of the game. I made the most of it. I pulled out every trick I knew at that time and it worked. I was lead comedian for more than two decades after that.

So who is this man Abe Saperstein? Each person who knew him, or knew of him, saw him differently.

In the time I knew him, the time I spent with him, I learned to love him. This doesn't mean I liked everything he did or said. I do know that Abe had a love for me and I appreciated him.

When there were only five black players in the NBA, Abe had more than 90 on his payroll. Abe loved sports, and he had a passion for NBA basketball. He owned 16% of the Philadelphia Warriors before they moved to the San Francisco area and became the Golden Gate Warriors. He had interests in major league baseball, too.

Abe gave me not only a job, he gave me a chance to fulfill my dream and see my vision come to reality. Abe helped me to live the American dream.

To me, no combination could compare with the teams we had in the late 1950s and early 1960s. The friendships, the laughs, the stories couldn't be topped. We used to go to the floor every night hungry and mad because of the tough lives we lived. If a guy scored against you and you suspected he had had a decent meal before the game, watch out! We had to love basketball to go through what we went through.

The toughest part about traveling with the Globetrotters was trying to understand Abe Saperstein. An inch or two taller than 5' and who knows how many pounds, he was about as different as he could be from his ballplayers. Most of us were tall, thin, and black. He was Jewish, and he smarted when people called him a slave owner or racist. He hired blacks when it was unfashionable, and he liked to think of us as his children. He used to say, "There are two things you can get fired for: not stopping to look at the basket and messing with my women."

Once in Paris, we led a team 56-0 with a second to go before the half. He loved that. It was a blowout! Then one of their players threw the ball from one end of the court to the basket at the opposite end. Miraculously, the ball went it! Abe was furious. We had let him down and embarrassed him. He liked to call us Oscars. I guess he was accusing us of acting.

The best game I ever played as a Globetrotter wasn't good enough for Abe. I must have scored about 50 points, played tough defense, and all my comedy bits had the crowd screaming. We won an interesting if not close game, and I glowed in the aftermath. I was called to Abe's hotel room. I just knew he was going to praise me, maybe even give me a raise, maybe slip me a few dollars for some fun. Instead, he ranted and raved about my game, my laziness, my slowness. He warned me that I had better pull my game together.

That was all I needed to hear. I was enraged to the point of tears. I would not let him see me break down. If he or I had said one more word in that room, I'd have popped him and we both would have cried.

I stormed out, determined to quit the team and go home. I called the airport. A flight to New York was scheduled for 9:00 the next morning. I reserved a seat.

I was packed and ready to go the next morning when I ran into Abe and a few of his friends. I decided not to say anything, to just nod and head for a taxi. I mourned the end of our relationship.

Abe caught my arm and introduced me to his friends. "And this, this is the best Globetrotter I've ever had. A super player, the consummate showman, a loyal team member, and a good friend, Meadowlark Lemon. We couldn't survive without him." He slipped me $100 and whispered, "Have yourself some fun tonight after the game, big guy."

You guessed it. I smiled, thanked him, went back to my room, unpacked, and had another great game that night – and some fun afterward.

Abe was a genius and a motivator. He handled all the promotion, made loans, and kept players from forming cliques by switching roommates whenever he felt it was necessary.

There were times when he might sidle up to a player after a game and slip $300 into his pocket. Once, on the bus to New London, Connecticut, after a game in Madison Square Garden, Abe produced two shopping bags full of cash and passed out bonuses to the players. I got about $500.

He taught me a lot of things. At the time, I didn't realize all that I learned from him or all the pressure he was under. He did what he had to do to put on the best possible show. I thought the team was it, the end-all, the show itself.

I didn't realize until I tried to put the Bucketeers, my own comedy basketball team, on the road how expensive it was and how many be-hind-the-scenes people it required. If they don't handle the business for you, you have no show.

I remember when the end was near for Abe. He fell asleep on the bench. I leaned over and put a hand on his shoulder. "You'd better go back to the hotel and get some sleep, Skip." He agreed, and he left. The last time I saw him was in his hotel lobby in Los Angeles. He told me how tired he was.

On March 15, 1966, I heard the phone ring at the scorers' table and knew it was bad news. "Skip has died. He would have wanted you to finish the game and the tour, and no one is expected to attend the funeral." That didn't seem right to me, although we abided by his wishes. We loved him. I know he died doing what he loved most, running the Harlem Globetrotters.

We were legitimate basketball players.

Back in the 1950s and 1960s, the Globetrotters played the College All-Stars every year. This event was bigger than the NCAA tournament or the NBA finals. For three weeks, we would tour the country and play against the best college players of the time. We played as many as 20 or 21 games in 19 nights!

The crowds were huge. We once had 32,000 in the Rose Bowl and 36,000 inside the Los Angeles Coliseum.

The college players were great: Bob Cousy, Bill Sharman, Tom Gola, Tommy Heinsohn, Frank Ramsey, and on and on. A lot of them went on to have success in the pros.

In 1950, the NBA started to draft black players, including Chuck Cooper, Sweetwater Clifton, and Earl Lloyd. Cooper and Sweetwater had been with the Globetrotters.

As a result, we started losing some of our best talent to the NBA. Even then, we were still the biggest game in town. Some people say that the Globetrotters kept the NBA in business in its early years.

Bob Cousy, who went on to become a legend with the Boston Celtics, once said that the NBA teams would schedule doubleheaders, with the Globetrotters playing against somebody in the first game and then two NBA teams playing in the second game. "The Globetrotters would sell out, but they'd always play the first game," Cousy said. "When they were through, half the house would get up and leave. So we knew what our position was."

I was always proud to
put on that uniform!

The NBA owners figured that out pretty fast, and made sure the Globetrotters would play in the nightcap so the fans wouldn't leave!

The Globetrotters were international stars. Our government called us "Ambassadors of Good Will in Short Pants." That didn't always give us much motivation, though, because we still traveled in parts of our own country where the white players on our opposing teams would go into the nice hotels and eat in the nice restaurants. We couldn't. One day, Abe Saperstein saw the pain in my face that this legacy of racism caused me. He said, "Mead, I know what you're going through. Mead, make 'em laugh." Those words helped change my life to one of seeking and giving joy.

It changed the way I saw my role. I had an opportunity to change the way people saw me. I had the ability to change the way I saw everyone else. It didn't have to be just about the color of our skin, white, black or any other color of the rainbow.

For this reason, my main contribution to the Globetrotters' legacy was my comedic prowess and basketball artistry. The comedy bits we called "reems." To this day, the Globetrotters refer to their ball tricks as "reems." That was what they were calling them when I joined. I have no idea what it means or how to spell it. Certain things just got handed down to you.

Along with my own clowning, I always liked the slapstick stuff that Jerry Lewis is famous for. And he inspired some of the stuff I worked into my act on the court. I loved Goose Tatum. I only saw him a few times. Bill Cosby made me laugh on his TV show when he was the dad of the Huxtables. Bill would come out with the Globetrotters

That's me pulling off a "reem." No one loved all the gags more than I did.

sometimes. We kept a uniform for Bill Cosby and for Wilt. Those were the only people we carried uniforms for. We didn't know when they might show up. It wasn't a publicity thing; they would just show up. Bill was around us quite a bit. He was inducted as part of the Globetrotters' team when we all went into the Hall of Fame.

Down through the years, the fans loved the way the basketball took on a personality of its own in our hands. The ball might suddenly decide on its own to begin to wobble and bounce sideways, making opponents scramble all over the floor. Or you might not be able to pass it at all; it'd snap right back to you every time. The ball would be there one minute, and gone the next. We could roll and glide that ball up one arm, around the back, and down the other arm. It didn't matter. We could do anything with it.

The Magic Circle was always done to the whistled tune
"Sweet Georgia Brown."

We always kept a bucket around. There are so many things you can do with a bucket. You might want to douse Curly Neal with freezing cold water. Sometimes I missed him, and got the audience with confetti. What happened to the water? It was a mystery to us all. If none of that was going on, we'd just hang out and play some football with the basketball. Maybe some baseball. The referees had a hard time keeping up, and I'm sure I had more home runs with a basketball than I ever did with a baseball. We had so much fun together. It was always different. It was always exciting

The incomparable Magic Circle, which was the classic warm-up performance accompanied by "Sweet Georgia Brown," showcased our love for the game, and each other. It looked like a party on the floor, because it was a party. The red, white, and blue uniforms, the smiles, the amazing athletes, the spirited basketball, these were my dreams come to life.

I already told you how much I liked to fake that my arm got hurt, and the other players would come over to me and rub my arm and make a big show out of my being injured. I would yell and carry on for a few minutes, and then I'd say, "It's my leg!" Man, that would bring the house down!

We had a million reems. In our football reem we would line up like football players in a formation and throw passes or do running plays. We would call a penalty on the other team and walk off five yards down the court. Sometimes, we'd play basketball like it was baseball with a pitcher, a batter, and outfielders. I loved doing that stuff. And the crowds loved it, too.

Here we are doing the fake arm injury. After minutes of my teammates nursing my arm, I would yell out, "It's my leg!"

Ballhandling was an important part of the Globetrotters' pre-game show. All of us could make that ball sing, dance, play peek-a-boo, and spin like a top!

One time, I was getting ready to shoot the ball, and this big dude hit me and knocked me to the floor. I didn't even think about what I was doing and I shot the ball between his legs. The ball hits the backboard and goes in. I started laughin' and he was chasing me around the court, he was so mad. It was during one of those College All-Star games we used to play every year.

A very famous episode happened in Columbus, Ohio, at the old fairgrounds there.

I don't know how this man got the seats he got. He had two chairs right under the basket. And he had this little kid who was laughing his socks off the whole game. Well, the ball got loose from me, and as I went to get it, I thought I'd have a little fun with this kid. I threw the ball to him, it hit him in the chest, and bounced back to me. I threw it again, same thing. I teased him: "Man, can't you catch?" The man says, "I'm his uncle and he's as blind as a bat. I've been telling him everything you're doing. That's why he's been laughing so hard."

Afterwards, I thought: "Wow! We can make a blind man see!"

Many years ago, the Globetrotters were playing in Ecuador, and for several days I couldn't sleep. I'd wake up early in the morning and walk the streets of Ecuador. One day I came across a cathedral. It was filled with candlelight. I remained there for a time. It was calm. It was cool. I finally relaxed. I decided to return to the hotel to get some sleep. That's when I heard belly-bursting laughter outside my window. I'd never heard anyone laugh quite like that before.

I looked out the window to see what was going on, and I saw a little girl running around in a circle, with someone chasing her. My eyes fixed on her. I noticed that her hair was matted into her scalp, and I wondered why her hair wasn't combed. The next thing I noticed was that she didn't have any arms. Then I noticed she didn't have any legs. Her legs looked like they were cut off above the knee and the stumps had leather tips on them. She was running and laughing. She had JOY in her life. We in America, we have everything. Many of us have no JOY. She had nothing and even then she had JOY.

One time, after we had finished playing three games in Houston, Texas, we were going to have a 500-mile bus trip the next day. We decided to drive half the distance right after our Sunday night game in Houston. We got on our bus and began cruising through the miles. We decided to stop for something to eat. As black Americans we couldn't eat in the local restaurants or even in the bus station restaurant. So we went to the back station window to order sandwiches. As the bus pulled up in front of the station, I was the first person out the door. A car pulled up in front of our bus. A man got out of the car with a blue-eyed, blonde-haired girl about 7 or 8 years old. She saw me and started laughing. She leaped from the man's arms, ran over to me, and began to hug and kiss me. She didn't see my color. She saw JOY. The man said, "Meadowlark, my daughter has never laughed like this in her life, and she's dying of a rare disease." She was laughing, he was crying, and I began to cry, too.

What a profound example of what we meant to all kinds of people.

As you know by now, my signature play – the one that Number 36 had to do every night – was the can't-miss half-court hook shot. As I talked about earlier, I've been practicing that hook shot since I was 11 years

There it is – the hook shot!
Thanks, Poppa Jack.

old. I could amaze crowds with my ability to sink hook shots. I'd walk away from the basket, not even looking, and flip the ball over my head for two points. Wilt Chamberlain said that he would be happy to make that shot just once. "You can't practice those things," he said. "How do you practice a once-in-a-lifetime shot, even though you're asked to make it every night? It's like practicing drowning."

"It's like there was a magnet drawing that shot into the basket."

I wonder how many hook shots I've tried in my life. I don't know if I can count that high.

The Globetrotters have played in 120 countries. They have covered the alphabet from Algeria to Zimbabwe. They have played more than 25,000 games. They play in front of two million people per year.

The team once played in an empty swimming pool in Germany because it was the largest available concrete surface in the whole area. The echo was unbelievable, not to mention the strange bounce on the gently sloping floor. There were games outdoors during a tour of France where it rained most of the time. We played on an aircraft carrier. (You had to be careful not to stray out-of-bounds on that court!)

I think it was about 1960, they built this new sports arena in Paris and the architect forgot to put dressing rooms and toilets in. So we dressed on the bus. In-between quarters and at halftime, we just sat on the sidelines.

One night, we had to use trash cans to catch rain water coming through the ceiling of our hotel room. I tell you, it wasn't always glamorous.

Most of the players had trouble with their feet and knees and hips and ankles. Playing 10 games in a week takes a terrible toll on the body.

I used an old-home remedy to take the swelling out of my knees: clay and vinegar.

The clay was like old, red Southern dirt-type clay. We would scoop some of that up off the roadside if we were playing in the South. If we were out of the country, we'd have to try to find some clay somewhere. If you couldn't, you just soaked towels in vinegar and wrapped them around your knees. And in the morning, the swelling would be down. And you would smell like vinegar.

Another time, I had dysentery in Egypt. Still played. Almost passed out a couple of times, and I still played. Other guys would fight through the flu and all sorts of bumps and bruises. You couldn't spend too much time worrying about it. You had to get ready for the next game because it was probably comin' tomorrow.

Over the years, the Globetrotters have played in over 100-degree heat and in below-zero cold. The team once played a game under martial law in Bogota, Colombia, in front of a crowd controlled by men with machine guns. They broke a backboard in Germany one day and had to play half-court ball. They broke another backboard in Belgium and duct-taped a coat hanger to a pole instead. That reminds me of my first home-made hoop.

In Italy, the team played on plywood sheets that covered an ice skating rink. It sleeted, and the boards separated. We kept warm by alternating five guys on the "floor" with five in the locker room every few minutes.

We played on soccer fields where we chalked off the basketball court so we wouldn't have to run the length of the field. We had to be ready on short notice to construct poles and backboards so the rims and nets could go up. We never knew what the surface would be.

In the south of France, we played in a bull ring (the longest distance between baskets ever – approximately 50 yards!) where we had to dribble through blood and other unmentionables. I remember playing on a clay tennis court when it rained and left us ankle deep in red stuff.

We put down a portable floor and fences so we could play on beaches in Italy. We had to find rocks and bags of dirt to secure the poles. After games like that, we didn't even shower and change until we had helped tear down the portable stadium.

The Globetrotters played on tennis courts in Bermuda, and on a ballroom dance floor in Germany that was so slippery they doused it with soda pop to make it sticky. They lit up a court with car lights in South America, and played right beside the ocean in the Bahamas.

We played in a bull ring one time in Europe and the promoter forgot to bring in baskets. So we made some baskets. We went out and got plywood and a saw and made a backboard, and found some old rims somewhere, and put these contraptions across from each other in this round bull ring. It ended up being twice as long as a basketball court. That was a long night.

That's me in a kilt, just one of a million outfits we wore as we traveled around the world.

When I was in the Army, we played a game in Germany. When we got there, there was no basketball floor. Somebody found some old wooden desks from the war. We put all them together and made a court out of these desks. They were big and heavy old things, so it worked out OK. You didn't even stub your toe in the gaps between the desks. Now, who goes and plays a basketball game on top of a bunch of old desks? There's some proof that the show must go on!

One time in Mexico, the Globetrotters were going to play in another bull ring. The local promoter wanted to add some pizzazz to the show, so he asked me – right before the basketball game – if I would be willing to fight a baby bull. I wasn't too sure about that. Sounded a little different than shooting a hook shot. They said "we will tape his horns up and make sure he can't hurt you." So, I'm a showman, right? The Clown Prince, right? Anything for the fans, right? I said OK.

Well, I found out that it was a baby bull, just like they said it would be. To my surprise, it wasn't a little bull. Just because a bull might be a baby doesn't mean he weighs less than 800 pounds!

They had its horns all taped up and they gave me the bull-fighter's red cape to wave at him and they sent me out into the ring. I waved the cape around a little bit, like I had seen real matadors do. And this baby bull came running at me. Fast. Snortin'. Spittin'. When he charged at me, my instincts took over. I didn't make a pretty pass with the cape. I didn't turn my back to him like the brave matadors do. I jumped over him. Yep. I jumped straight over his head and ran to the other end. I ran up into the stands scared out of my sneakers. The crowd was loving it because they thought it was part of the show. They didn't realize that this "reem" wasn't one I had ever thought about before. Thank God I was a young man then and still had my jumping legs!

Keep in mind, the Globetrotters played for popes, presidents, kings, and queens.

I became very close to one president, in particular. After I became an ordained minister, I was able to pray with President Ronald Reagan and Vice President (George H.W.) Bush. This was at a time when there was an initiative for prayer in schools, and a group of us were there. One of our group said, "Why don't we all go pray with President Reagan?" Somebody else said, "We can't! You have to plan these things way in advance." Somebody else said, "Do you know you have one of the greatest basketball players of all time with you, and Rosey Grier, one of the (Los Angeles Rams') Fearsome Foursome? He'll want to talk to these people!"

My team, the Shooting Stars, honored First Lady Nancy Reagan with her own jersey.

So we got to pray with President Reagan that very day for our nation.

We went there (to the White House) to bless him personally, not for any particular decision he was facing or any particular issue. When we prayed, there were tears in Reagan's eyes. He loved our country. You could tell he really appreciated it.

I make it a part of my daily routine to pray for this country and its leaders. They need our prayers. They committed to serve our country, and I will do my part as a citizen and servant to the United States to remember this is one nation, under God, indivisible, with liberty and justice for all.

I could never imagine what a president goes through on a daily basis. I don't see how he survives with all these important decisions he has to make. We must pray for and bless our presidents no matter who they are.

I was working with First Lady Nancy Reagan, too. Our basketball team helped with her "Just Say No" to drugs project. We went into all these schools on our own dime to support her cause because we believed in it. We asked the government for nothing. I know she appreciated that.

President Reagan was at some big fund-raiser event, and he and Nancy were up on the stage with Bob Hope. Well, Nancy sees me sitting down in the first couple of rows, and she runs off the stage, leaps into my arms, and gives me a big hug. Bob Hope says, "Who is that?" President Reagan says, "Oh, that's just Meadowlark." Bob Hope says, "Yeah, I know him."

I've had a blessed life. I am the American Dream.

I was blessed to have a close relationship with President Ronald Reagan.

I came back to the White House to pray with the first George Bush when he became president. He was asking us about being born-again Christians, and he said, "I guess I've been born again all my life!"

We played before two popes – Pope Paul and Pope John. It was like the heavens opened up when this man, the pope, watched us do our little basketball thing that we do. Both of them blessed us. Those were great honors in my life.

Another time, we were in Brussels, Belgium, for about 10 days. We played in Antwerp and all around that area. One day, we're in the gym and we hear this noise, like an earthquake. And this king and 10 of his wives – he had a hundred of them – and about 100 of his soldiers burst into the gym to watch us play. The "earthquake" we heard was the sound of the soldiers marching. It was one of the most fantastic things I have ever experienced.

Years later, when I had become a minister, I was going to visit a prison in Louisiana. I was accompanied by a pastor by the name of Denny Duran from Shreveport. A man in his church, named Bud, had taken a liking to me. Some of the members of the church liked to kid me; they would say, "You'd better watch Bud because he's the head of the Ku Klux Klan."

Well, Bud picked me up from the airport to drive me to this prison. It seemed like we would never get there, driving through long stretches of backwoods. Bud asked me if I would like something to drink and I said yes. So we stopped at a service station. While I was getting an orange pop to drink, this man came out of the back room of the station. He was wearing blue-and-white overalls, with one shoulder strap unhooked and hanging off his shoulder.

He looked at me and said, "Meadows, is that you?"

I said, "Yes, sir," and he began to hug me.

He said, "You have brought so much joy to me and my family."

I thanked him and we got back in Bud's car. Bud asked me, "What are you? I know these people. They don't like black people, but they love you! What are you?"

That's the kind of impact we had.

Through the years, the Globetrotters' opponents were some of the best in basketball ... the Washington Generals, the Kansas City All-Stars, the House of David, the Boston Whirlwinds, the Honolulu Surf Riders, and the Philadelphia SPHAs (South Philadelphia Hebrew Association).

And, of course, we played the college all-star teams and several foreign countries' Olympic basketball teams.

I loved it all.

My friend Mannie Jackson, who is an owner of the Globetrotters and who also was a player on the team back in the early 1960s, said, "Meadowlark is the original live Showtime."

That's quite a compliment, and I'm grateful for it.

Our president, Barack Obama, is a basketball fan. He once said, "When the Globetrotters came to town, it was a wonderful, joy-filled afternoon. But I think it had a deeper meaning to it."

It did have a deeper meaning. It meant fun. It meant progress. It meant pride. And it was done out of love.

S Spirit

H Health

O Opportunity

T Teamwork

SECOND HALF

Trust Your Next S.H.O.T.

S.H.O.T. – A Guide to a Life of Joy

We're comin' out after halftime of this book. I had an incredible first half of my journey. I don't mind telling the story. It's an amazing story. I'm still living it. It's still amazing. I know what I'm talking about when I tell you this secret to life – love what you do and do it with all the joy it deserves. It's not that there won't be challenges along the way. There definitely will be. Plan in advance; your vision will carry you through those times. Keep your mind on the hope you hold in your heart. Please always remember, life's most meaningless statistic is the half-time score.

SECOND HALF
Trust Your Next S.H.O.T.

When I travelled the world entertaining and giving it my all for the fans, it was the connection I felt with the audiences, the joyful connection that I still notice between us when I'm on the road, that fueled my energy to do my best over and over again. Even after you've given everything you've got in your first half, the game is still going on. You've got to be able to trust your next shot! That's the title of this book, and it's also a way to think about living a life overflowing with joy. Some of you may think you're in your fourth quarter right before the buzzer is going to go off. As far as I'm concerned, it's always half-time.

My story is about faith. It's also about trust. Trust that YOU can have a life of joy. You're more than a survivor. You're an overcomer. We are all sent here to Earth with an assignment from the Creator. Despite what you may have seen so far, you were sent here for such a time as this. Everything you need to accomplish your assignment is already inside of you. Take the shots that matter the most to you, and believe that you will make them.

If you have prepared thoroughly ...

If you have practiced every day ...

If you have memorized the basics and given your best effort every day in every way ...

Then you will have the confidence to trust your next shot.

It's goin' in – you've gotta believe that you just can't miss.

I've taken too many shots to count in practices and games through the years. And I've made my share of shots. The very word itself – "SHOT" has been important in my life.

It should be important in your life, too. I like to keep things simple, and stick to the fundamentals. I'll make it easy for you to remember the basics of an extraordinary life. Think of the word "SHOT" as representing Spirit, Health, Opportunity, and Teamwork. I will share with you the best information I have at this time, from an ordinary person who lives an extraordinary life, and it will be up to you to take your best shot.

"*Excellence is an art won by training and habituation. We do not act rightly because we have virtue or excellence, but rather we have those because we have acted rightly. We are what we repeatedly do. Excellence, then, is not an act but a habit.*"

– Aristotle

Chapter
11

"S" Means Spirit

The **"S"** in SHOT stands for Spirit.

I like to think about spirit in several different ways. Your spirit is your soul. It's your way of being in the world. It's your source of energy and enthusiasm. It's where love comes from. It's where strength comes from. We like to say of certain people, "They have a strong spirit."

Spirit is our inner self. It is the connected mind, emotions, and will. Everything happens in our inner self first, before it can be manifested in the world. It's important to deal with our spirit first. Everything we see on the outside of a person was cultivated on the inside. When I'm asked to teach my hook shot, I'll say that the shot comes from the inside out.

The first time I landed one of those shots in a game, everyone would call it luck. After seven or eight from all over the court, everyone would call it magic. The truth is, this shot was a gift from God to me. I always felt like it was evidence of God's creation. My ability to make that shot was an expression of my spirit. My gift is that hook shot, first *received* by me from God, then in turn given by me as a gift to millions.

Spirit is the source of passion. It is the burning love that fuels your life's work. When I was 11 years old, I began to practice basketball six, eight, sometimes 10 hours a day. I couldn't get enough of it. When I was first learning how to shoot a hook shot, I would go for a half-hour at a time without even hitting the backboard. Then I would go for another hour without hitting the rim. And another hour before one shot would trickle through the net.

I never gave up or got frustrated because my spirit and passion for the game kept burning bright inside me. And, by the way, I played in more than 16,000 consecutive games. I'd say my spirit played a major part in that accomplishment.

I believe that life is fullest when we spend some time every single day engaging in our passion. I still do basketball drills every day. I keep in shape so I can play well for my current team, Meadowlark Lemon's Harlem All-Stars.

We all were created by God. We all get to enjoy the blessings of life and the abundance of this world, no matter where we start out in life. We all need guidance, and it is said, "When the student is ready the teacher will show up." When I speak of blessing and abundance, be sure to realize knowledge and experience are rich blessings.

Living without spirit is living empty. And as imperfect human beings, we tend to fill empty spaces in our lives with unhealthy things – alcohol, drugs, pornography, greed, bad relationships, too much work.

Today, I am a preacher and
teacher of God's grace.

Traveling over all the corners of the earth, you observe many things and many people. And seemingly ordinary people can and do accomplish extraordinary things.

Life is not measured by what you possess; it's measured by what possesses you. I have known most of the luxuries money can afford and the admiration that comes with fame.

I have been called the Clown Prince of Basketball, and an Ambassador of Good Will in Short Pants to the world, which is an honor.

To be a child of God is the highest honor anyone could have.

Spirit and Heart

Heart is both physical and spiritual.

It's no secret that people recognize you by the output of your heart. You may be known as "half hearted," "whole-hearted," or even a "heartache." The person who is in the best position to grab that rebound or make that free throw in life is the one who can forget about their own challenges for awhile and show concern for the needs of others around him.

Poppa Jack is one of the best examples of a "wholehearted" individual. He brought his heart to work with him every day when he worked with kids who may have seemed insignificant in the eyes of others.

Put Your Heart into It!

Have you ever heard someone say, *"Put your heart into it?"* Or *"Give it your whole heart?"* I remember hearing a quote, "Do well even the most tedious job and when the day is over, there will be no regrets, no time wasted. Then joy will come." There is an **inner joy** when we have done the best we can. I had joy knowing that I had done my best in every game I played, regardless of the size of the crowd. I never felt that I had to be as good as or better than someone else. I always knew I was only in competition with myself: "Could I play a little bit better than my last game or get a bigger laugh from the crowd?" Doing something with your **"whole heart"** means giving it the best you can offer. As long as I knew I did my best, I felt a sense of accomplishment and *joy.*

Heart can mean having courage and staying power or what some of my buddies and I might say, "That took a lot of guts!" It took a lot of heart, spirit, and guts to play in 16,000 professional basketball games all over the world. We played in all kinds of weather conditions with no guarantee of a place to eat or sleep, except for on our bus. Sometimes, we traveled untold hours without stopping so we could dash into an arena and bring joy and laughter to fans who may have been waiting there for hours. For the love of the game and the joy it brought to us as a team – it was all worth it.

"When the Globetrotters came to town, it was a wonderful, joy-filled afternoon. But I think it had a deeper meaning to it."

– President Barack Obama

Even Fools the Boss. Meadowlark Lemon, new comedy sensation of the Harlem Globetrotters, unleashes a bit of his tomfoolery on Owner-Coach Abe Saperstein.

Wearing the Globetrotters uniform always made me smile.

Here I am celebrating my 3,000th game.

I was honored and blessed to meet the Pope.

Meadowlark Lemon – Crown Prince of Basketball

Serious at the moment in an airplane card game is Meadowlark Lemon, celebrated comedian of the Harlem Globetrotters basketball team.

A Stroll in West Berlin –
Taking in the sights during 1961
Harlem Globetrotters Tour

(Right) Some of the
Globetrotters, including
me, took in the sites
in Europe with
Abe Saperstein,
the team's owner.

Harlem Globetrotters' Meadowlark Lemon lunches aboard aircraft carrier
Enterprise, off San Francisco, after an exhibition for Navy men.

I'm with my wife, Cynthia, at a black-tie event.

I'm second from the left as me and four of my teammates perform on the Ed Sullivan Show.

I'm SO pretty!

(Above) On air with baseball legend Joe Garagiola.

The shot that made me famous: the long-distance hook!

Now you see me...

Here are a few of us on a television soundstage. The fellow with the "high-water pants" (third from right) is comedian Bill Cosby. We always kept a uniform ready for him in case he showed up to play.

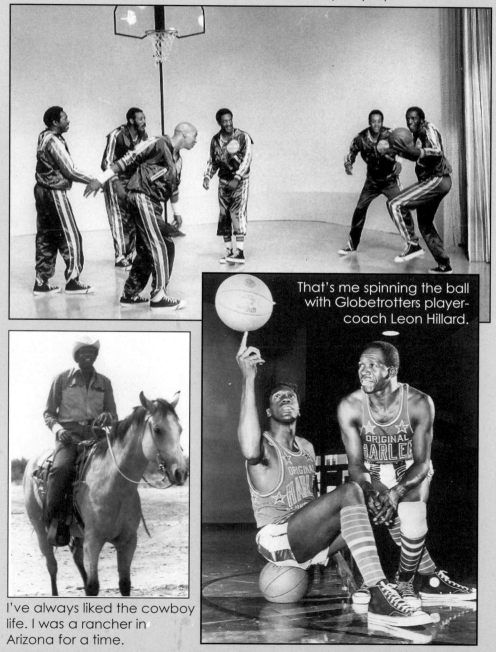

That's me spinning the ball with Globetrotters player-coach Leon Hillard.

I've always liked the cowboy life. I was a rancher in Arizona for a time.

This is probably how Meadowlark looks to audiences – and opponents –
as the Harlem Globetrotters' popular Crown Prince sets up tricky routines
for the basketball magicians.

Globetrotters' Meadowlark Lemon finds a "rival" in San Francisco.

That's me with my biggest teammate, Wilt "The Big Dipper" Chamberlain.
Wilt holds the career record for rebounds in the history of the NBA.

Here I am with Heavyweight Champ
Joe Louis, Abe Saperstein, and Jay
North, TV star Dennis the Menace.

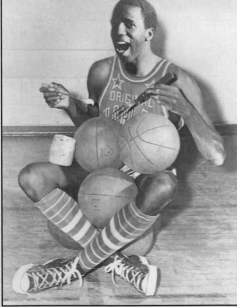

He's done everything but eat
basketballs and now Globetrotters'
Meadowlark Lemon tries that.

That's the "Greatest"– Muhammad
Ali – with me at the Ebony Sports
50th Anniversary Celebration.

"Baby" Curly and Uncle Meadowlark on the TV show *The Popcorn Machine*.

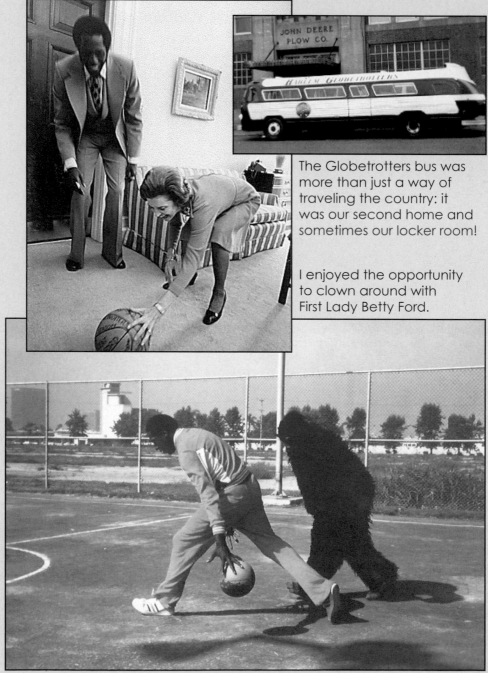

The Globetrotters bus was more than just a way of traveling the country: it was our second home and sometimes our locker room!

I enjoyed the opportunity to clown around with First Lady Betty Ford.

I have played against ALL KINDS of players!

Chapter
12

"H" Means Health

The **"H"** in SHOT stands for Health.

I have always made exercise and taking care of my body a priority. People ask me how I stay so healthy and physically fit. They want to know how I've been able to have such longevity in my career, especially how I'm still playing basketball with my team, Meadowlark Lemon's Harlem All Stars, at events all over the country.

I know there are lots of kids watching my life. I tell them they don't have to take drugs, or drink or smoke, to be somebody. The things you have to give up are the things that are killing you, anyway. Thomas Edison was quoted as saying, "The doctor of the future will interest his patient in the care of the human frame, in diet and in the cause and prevention of disease."

I'm on the road 80% of the time. My schedule is full as a keynote speaker and as a guest speaker at many churches. I also participate in many celebrity fundraisers and other events with my comedy basketball team. I conduct Camp Meadowlark basketball camps and clinics, I make other personal appearances, and I do collaborative work with our outreach to Native Americans. My office is always full of activity with opportunities for me to consider and meetings to attend when I'm off the road. Also, I love spending time with my family. It's in my best interest to choose to stay healthy and fit by making healthy daily choices. It takes perseverance to show up at all these events on my schedule with the kind of energy people expect from me and I expect from myself. I'm

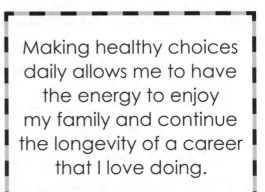

Making healthy choices daily allows me to have the energy to enjoy my family and continue the longevity of a career that I love doing.

thankful and grateful that I have the energy and health to keep up with my schedule. Making healthy choices daily allows me to have the energy to enjoy my family and continue the longevity of a career that I love doing. I enjoy what I do – it brings me JOY.

I learned at the beginning of my career that health affects everyone physically, mentally, spiritually, financially, socially, and emotionally. Unhealthy people miss work and may lose money, which in turn affects them financially and spiritually. They may not have the energy for family and friends; this affects them socially, which in turn affects them mentally, and they get depressed. One unhealthy person in a family can affect the whole family in a negative way. I could see that people who were taking care of their bodies by making healthy choices on a daily basis were much happier and more productive in their lives. It's clear to see that it's easier to maintain a healthy body and resist disease than try to fix the challenge with drugs, surgeries, or many visits to doctors. It's also clear to me that no one else can take care of my body for me and if my body breaks down there is no amount of money that can turn things around. It would take tremendous effort to become well again. It takes effort to stay well. Either way, it takes effort on our part to maintain health and vitality. I would much rather spend my time and money taking care of my healthy body. I always want to enjoy and take great care of my family and my career. By keeping the maintenance of my health at the top of my priority list, I can do everything I want to do. My family tells me they appreciate how I take care of myself, and they see my love for them in the commitment I make to my own health.

I'm careful with the foods I choose to eat. There is no food that is worth taking a chance that it may affect my body in a negative way. If I'm not sure about a particular food or beverage, I use this tried and tested rule: when in doubt – don't.

So, "How do I stay so healthy and fit and how do I know what to do?" My first step is to get the assistance of my MVP, also known as my wife, Dr. Cynthia Lemon. She is a naturopathic doctor with a double doctorate in nutritional philosophy. Naturopathic medicine focuses on holistic, proactive prevention. Instead of waiting for a disease to emerge, Naturopathic doctors work to head it off before it happens. She works with patients to improve health through diet, supplementation, exercise and holistic and non-drug remedies. She designed a program that works for me and has worked for over 17 years. I am going to share with you some of the fundamental basic things that I do each day.

There are a lot of things we can't control, like the air we breathe and the weather. We *can* control what we put into our mouths and what we feed to our children.

We can learn a lot about the benefits from healthy eating from Daniel in the Bible. He knew the importance of a healthy diet, and he proved it was worthwhile to choose well. When he was a young man, just a teenager, the king told his officials to find the strongest, healthiest, most intelligent young men to serve in his court. Daniel was chosen. The officials were instructed to feed these young men with the king's rich, fancy foods and to give them plenty of wine. The king wanted them to be the strongest and healthiest they possibly could be.

Daniel was a breed apart. Since he knew some of those foods had been offered up to idols and he knew many of them were not good for him, he told the official, "I don't want to eat this food. Just give me fresh vegetables and water."

The official didn't know what to think. Finally, he said, "All right Daniel. We'll let you try this for a little while. In a few days, we're going to see how you compare to these other young men."

Ten days later, the Bible says, Daniel was stronger, healthier, and 10 times smarter than the other young men. He had God's blessings and he was also putting the correct fuel into his body. While the other guys were drinking lots of wine and eating unhealthy food, Daniel was filling up on nutritious foods. My family refers to this type of diet as a "Daniel Fast," and at the first of every year for many years now, I do this fast along with my wife so we can get a healthy start on the new year. You should try it sometime. It can be for one day or as many days as you decide. You'll feel refreshed.

We use common sense approaches. We eat organic food whenever possible. We read labels – the closer the food is to its original form and the fewer additives it contains, the higher quality of food it will be. We look for foods that are not genetically modified and foods that are fresh rather than packaged. I like organic raw nuts for snacks. We have a lot of organic grains and organic lentils and beans. One of my favorite organic breads is called Ezekiel Bread and the recipe came from the Bible. It's higher in protein than other whole grain breads.

We only eat meats that are recommended in the Bible (Leviticus, Chapter 11 and Deuteronomy, Chapter 14) because medical science has proven the Bible to be true. We make sure all the meat and eggs we use are organic and hormone- and drug-free. That means no pork or shellfish; we only eat fish with fins and scales. On the rare occasion that we eat red meat, we make sure it's organic and grass fed.

Everyone already knows that the use of drugs, alcohol, and cigarettes and being overweight eventually causes disease. Sometimes, health comes more by what you stop doing; so stop putting things in your body that you already know are harmful.

We like to use some common things that are found in nature, things God made that have been proven through centuries to be beneficial in keeping our bodies healthy.

I supplement my diet with the items on this list:

- Braggs Raw Apple Cider Vinegar
- Organic Cold-Pressed Aloe Vera Juice
- Organic Greens
- Organic Chlorophyll
- Organic Calcium with Vitamin D
- Organic Strontium
- Cod-Liver Oil (wild caught)
- Organic Coconut Oil
- Organic Acidophilus
- Purified water daily – ½ my body weight is the daily recommended amount I use (more when I'm on the golf course or the basketball court)
- Fresh-Squeezed Lemon Juice in about 20 ounces of my daily water that I alternate throughout the day with my purified water. The recipe I use:
  - *18 ounces of purified water mixed with 2 ounces of fresh squeezed-lemon and 2 tablespoons of organic pure maple syrup or organic raw honey*

You can get a detailed explanation of the many benefits found uniquely in each one from various sources, including the internet. Remember though, while everyone is their own best doctor, check with your family doctor before making any major changes in your daily routine. No one knows more about your body than you do. Many people get sick due to a lack of knowledge. There is so much knowledge freely offered on the internet and in your local library. I'm blessed to have a wife who is also my doctor. Now you need to be interested in your health enough to put some effort into seeking knowledge. I've given you a place to start; the rest is up to you. Seek and you shall find!

I still exercise every day and get plenty of fresh air and sunshine. My training at the gym starts with stretching exercises to increase my flexibility and get my muscles warmed up before I do any weight lifting or basketball practice. I sometimes jog around the gym to increase my heartbeat and blood circulation.

Now it's time to step onto the basketball court to shoot some hoops. When I step over the painted black baseline and onto the playing court, a change comes over me.

I always include my fundamental shooting drills in my training. When I'm on the court, I'm concentrating so intensely that nothing else exists.

And, yes, a lot of the time I'm working on the hook shot. It still goes in – as can be verified by some of those half my age who have attempted to block the shot.

I warm up by shooting it from about 10 feet. Then I move out to maybe 15-16 feet. I move to the corner of the court, about 20 feet out, and make it 10 times in a row from that spot. Finally, I move out to near center court and swish in several from there.

Sometimes I challenge myself. If the basketball touches the rim – even if the shot goes through the net – it doesn't count. It was a few inches off from being perfectly aimed and, as a result, I don't count it. I force myself to start my shooting streak over again.

I have often been told that a smile pops up on my face every time I shoot that hook shot. I don't do it on purpose. People have shown me pictures, and, sure enough, I am smiling. It's no secret I have a good time on the basketball court.

To finish off my workout, I do cool-down stretching for five or 10 minutes.

My routine takes about an hour and it's a necessary part of my day. When I take that hour for myself, I can honestly say that I'm more energized and the rest of my day is much more productive. It reminds me of what airline flight attendants say at the beginning of every flight I am on, "In the event there is an emergency that requires the use of the oxygen mask, parents are to position their oxygen masks first before assisting their children." You need to take care of yourself first so that you can take care of your children.

Several times during the year, I do a cleanse, including fasting, and I keep a positive mental attitude and expect good things to come my way every day. Worry is a misuse of the imagination! I get up every day and thank God for the good things he's sending my way and for all the blessings I already have. I live a life of gratitude. It is written in Proverbs, "A merry heart does good like a medicine ..." That proverb has been proven by experience and now medical studies back it up, too. Modern medical research has proven that getting patients to laugh for extended periods of time each day lessens pain and depression, which, in turn, decreases the amount of pain medications and anti-depressants needed by the patient. All from adding laughter to their daily routine. They tell their patients to take time to laugh and play and enjoy the life God has given them by watching some funny movies or cartoons or by playing with their kids. Just find something that makes you laugh.

There is healing power in laughter. When you have a joyful spirit, health and healing are flowing. Some doctors recommend that at least three times daily, we should find something funny that makes us laugh out loud. Not a quiet laugh on the inside. Every time you laugh, it boosts your immune system. It reduces your blood pressure. Tension leaves and creativity comes. If you'll stay on this prescription and laugh every day with a happy heart, having a cheerful mind, then you're going to sleep better. You're going to get more done. You'll have more energy. You're going to make better decisions. You'll be more creative. You may even see some of these areas of pain, fatigue, and depression begin to go away.

Many believe they don't have time to focus on their health. The truth is if you don't make the time yourself, someone else will do it for you. Many think it's either all or nothing. The truth is it's a daily process of gradual adjustments. Men don't decide their future. They decide their habits, and then their habits decide their future. Ask yourself how much better would you feel if you exercised and ate healthier foods one day a week? How much better would you feel if you did the same thing two days a week? Every week you add an extra day. Maybe you can only exercise for 5 or 10 minutes a day – the important thing is that you start somewhere. If you backslide a few days – don't worry about it, just get right back on your healthy choice journey. It's not what you do from Thanksgiving to New Year's Day that makes the difference; it's what you do from New Year's Day to Thanksgiving that makes the bigger difference.

Everyone has a few off days and no one is perfect. Never give up – success is just a thought away. Change your thoughts to, "I can do this – I don't know how – I just know I can." At that moment, everything will start to change, even though there may be no obvious evidence. The evidence will come and you and others will begin to notice a better you. Focus on how good you're going to feel as you get stronger and healthier every day in every way. The important thing is that you take time for yourself, and you enjoy it. You are valuable and you are worth the time and energy it takes to be healthy.

I've also learned to handle stress in a healthier way. Everyone has stress; it's how we deal with stress that makes the difference. I choose to believe that regardless of the circumstances, everything always works out for me. I may not know how everything will work out based on the facts around me; I just believe that ultimately everything will turn around and my family and I will be OK.

When you have a choice, choose well the foods you are eating and the beverages you are drinking and see to your rest. If you've done all you can, even then sometimes tragic things happen. If you or someone you know has ever been involved in a terrible accident of some kind, you know the drastic changes it can make in your life. In those times it's absolutely crucial to Trust Your Next Shot. Even these things can be turned around for your good. I've asked my wife, Cynthia, to share her story, in her own words. I've repeated it many times over the years. It illustrates exactly what I mean.

This is a story my wife tells that happened just over a year before I met her:

I was driving down the freeway in a borrowed classic Cadillac about 50 miles per hour in St. Petersburg, Florida. My three-year-old daughter, Crystal, was strapped into her seatbelt in the back seat. Another car came out of nowhere, crossed the entire freeway, and hit me on the front driver's side of the Cadillac. It forced the car into a spin that spanned several lanes, eventually smashing into a telephone pole. It happened so fast. I vividly remember the sound of crushing metal. I was surprised that I didn't go through the window of the fast food restaurant in front of me. The telephone pole had stopped my car from crashing through that fast food restaurant, where the walls were mostly glass. I felt the pain that shot down my arms from my clenching grip on the steering wheel and also the pain that shot through my legs from the dashboard crushing my knees. I couldn't turn around to see my little daughter in the back seat. My first words were to my daughter, asking if she was OK. "Yes, Mommy, I'm OK."

At that time, it was not a law to have children strapped into a car seat. The day before the accident, Crystal had been riding in the front seat when I'd tapped the brakes to stop at a light and she had slid off the front seat. I decided she'd have to ride with a seat belt in the backseat from then on. Had she been in the front seat with me the day of the accident, she would have been killed.

The accident occurred before it was common for everyone to have a cell phone. Fortunately, miraculously, there were two police cars and an ambulance on the road next to me. They were right on the scene with no time to waste. A police officer looked after Crystal while they put a brace on my neck, pulled me from the wreck, and placed me on a gurney. I will always be thankful for that policeman who held my daughter and comforted her. I was in shock, and was being treated in the ambulance. My little girl was so brave, until she saw me in a neck brace and strapped down. All I could hear was her asking, "Who's going to take care of me?"

I had felt a strong compulsion to begin to pray about five minutes before the accident. I began praying while driving down the road. It was rush-hour traffic around 5:30 in the evening with people coming home from work, and I did not know why I wanted to pray – I just did it – and was praying aloud when the car struck us. The insurance company went out to take photos of the accident, and no one was able to locate a telephone pole at the site of the accident (although the crunched metal of the hood was clear proof there was a pole to stop us from going through the restaurant window).

In the hospital emergency room, I couldn't feel my legs. There was testing and X-rays and all the normal ER stuff. My daughter Angela (15) got a phone call from the nursing staff and had a friend bring her right over. She took Crystal home with her, and once I was alone, I finally cried. I wondered if I'd walk ever again. How would my children react to this? As a single mom and provider, what now? Again, would I walk? Could I carry my little one anymore? Was I OK? Why wasn't any of the ER staff giving me any information? I wondered what I was going to do about my own patients who needed me at the clinic? I had patients scheduled six months in advance. Who was going to teach my class at the John Robert Powers modeling school that I worked at three days a week? I was expected to show up and teach at the health spa that I also worked at part time - what would I do? Tears filled my eyes as I thought of my children. What if I would have just taken another way home or left a few minutes earlier or later? All the fears of 'now what?' began to flood my mind. Then I remembered I was impressed to pray just minutes before the accident. Since I had been a little girl growing up in the church, I'd "gotten saved" at least 10 or 15 times. Whenever there was an altar call I went up just to make sure I 'got it.' Suddenly I felt a peace surround me while I lay there motionless. I became thankful and grateful that I was alive, and that Crystal was alive and not hurt at all. I became thankful and grateful that today was the day she started wearing her seatbelt and riding in the backseat. God had prepared us in advance. Come what may, God was with us.

Eventually, I completed all the testing with the specialists. I could feel my toes. Good news. I wasn't paralyzed; I just had two totally crushed knee caps and severe ligament and cartilage damage. I referred all my patients to another naturopathic doctor and closed my office. I quit teaching at the modeling school and the health spa, thereby eliminating all sources of income. We exhausted the physical therapy options. I was prescribed many kinds of pain killers. The last doctor they sent me to was a pain specialist who was to wean me off the pain medications and teach me to live with the pain. They said I would have to learn to live with much pain. They said I would never walk without the use of knee braces and crutches. We lived on the third floor of a beautiful complex in Florida with no elevator. To get to each appointment, I had to be carried up and down three flights of stairs. My legs had to be straight, not bent, so the process was tricky.

I learned of the faithfulness of God in this time. My first night back home from the hospital I did one of those "Let the bible fall open, point your finger, and see what it says right there." The spot ended up being Matthew chapter 6:25-34. "Therefore I tell you, do not worry about your life, what you will eat or drink; or about your body, what you will wear. Is not life more important than food, and the body more important than clothes? Look at the birds of the air; they do not sow or reap or store away in barns, and yet your heavenly Father feeds them. Are you not much more valuable than they? Who of you by worrying can add a single hour to his life? And why do you worry about clothes? See how the lilies of the field grow. They do not labor or spin. Yet I tell you that not even Solomon in all his splendor was dressed like one of these. If that is how God clothes the grass of the field, which is here today and tomorrow is thrown into the fire, will he not much more clothe you, O you of little faith? So do not worry, saying, 'What shall we eat?' or 'What shall we drink?' or 'What shall we wear?' For the pagans run after all these things, and your heavenly Father knows that you need them. Seek first his kingdom and his righteousness, and all these things will be given to you as well. Therefore do not worry about tomorrow, for tomorrow will worry about itself. Each day has enough trouble of its own."

We relied on that promise. We saw miracles every day that encouraged my faith and let me know God knew me and my kids, and what we needed. He delighted us with provision in so many creative, unexpected ways. Oddly enough during that time, we gave to others more than we'd ever dreamed possible. Giving is joy. My amazing daughter, Angela, had a grace about her and a confidence about her to step in and manage so many very grown-up things. She was a great blessing and help to me and I am so thankful for her. Because of the hard work and teamwork, we have a strong bond to this day. It gives me joy to see, now 18 years later with a seven-year-old daughter of her own, her confidence in living that life of faith with the same enthusiasm and grace that we learned as a team together so many years ago. I'd also read that Jesus paid for my healing. Whenever anyone asked how I was, I would answer, "I'm getting better and better every day in every way." I'd tell my children to keep an eye on me because I'm about to get healed! This went on for nearly a year.

We heard on a local Christian TV program that a missionary from South Africa named Rodney Howard-Browne was holding healing crusades in a town almost two hours away. There were so many people being healed, they said, and so many miracles happening during the crusade that people were flying in from all over the country to check it out. The meetings were being held nightly and we began to go every day we could. The services would last late into the evening with more than 10,000 people there. Awesome things would happen. I was carried up the stairs on one of those nights to be prayed for – and without any lightning or thunder – I received brand new knee caps and total knee repair in both legs immediately. The pain was gone. I could walk. I walked down those stairs. I walked back up those stairs. Down again. Up again. Over and over. I drove us home that night. It was the first time in almost exactly one year that I'd driven. You have to know we were screaming and shouting and laughing all the way home. It was a celebration! I did not need any more pain medication. Our home economy changed in one day. If God did that for us, he will do it for you, too.

That was in March 1993. I had an opportunity to go to Arizona and teach at a college and see some local patients. Since the possibilities were wide open, I decided to go for three months. We found a home church with Pastor Michael Maiden and his family almost immediately after we arrived. We loved it and decided to stay a few more months. Before we had a chance to return home to Florida, I met Meadowlark at that same *church we loved. Three months after we met, we were married and we blended our families. We now have a child together named Caleb Lark Lemon, and looking back I'm thankful for that year I had to learn to live by faith and practice using my faith every day. I got a vision of my healing when I heard it was possible and I chose to stay focused on the vision and not on the daily circumstances. I saw myself walking around perfectly. I lived and spoke as if I were in only a temporary situation.*

God's miracles are a free gift to us. We all can have them. They're not unlike Meadowlark's thoughts on "free throws." They're free! As my amazing husband also says all the time – because it is so very true – preparation is power and perfect practice makes perfect.

So as you can see from Cynthia's story, we all have a journey to take. There will be choices and lessons and adversity along the way. Joy is not the absence of adversity. It is a victorious way through adversity. Remember what Abe Saperstein told me? Abe said, "Make 'em laugh, Mead." Now I say to you, "You make 'em laugh!" You can find in your *SPIRIT* as you walk in *HEALTH* the courage to look for an *OPPORTUNITY* and be a part of a *TEAM* that changes your life.

When

you get

a chance,

make

a play."

– Marques Haynes'
instructions from
the bench as I took
the court during my
tryout with the
Globetrotters

Chapter
13

"O" Means Opportunity

The **"O"** in SHOT stands for Opportunity.

Life is a series of opportunities. We take advantage of some of them; we miss many others. You know the old saying, "When opportunity knocks, answer." And when you do answer, if you have prepared for the opportunity, that preparation is power. You'll be ready for the test ahead of you.

When God opens doors, no man can shut them! One of the Psalms says, "God surrounds us with favor."

I was given the most wonderful opportunity of my life when the Globetrotters asked me to play on a team that was traveling across Europe.

The owner of the Globetrotters was Abe Saperstein, a white Jewish man just over five feet tall who was building a thriving business featuring the basketball talents of a team of black men. A time when blacks were not given a lot of opportunities by whites.

So, I jumped at the opportunity Mr. Saperstein gave me, and I made the most of it. Who knows how my life would have turned out if I hadn't practiced for the tryout with the Globetrotters. Would Marques Haynes have even bothered to mention what he'd seen to Abe Saperstein? What if I'd never made my own basket? What if all I did was go home and complain because I had no basket or basketball? How far could I have gone without preparing?

The opportunity came seven years after I had that dramatic experience at the Ritz Theater. I was tested and tried before 15,000 screaming Globetrotter fans. I was nervous at first, and then when I walked on the floor, it felt comfortable. After all, I had lived this moment every day for seven years. I had practiced continuously, daily, perfectly.

There were opportunities to fail along the way. One day at the Boys Club, two friends tried to get me to leave because we didn't like how the management and owners ran the club. We didn't know much about anything then, let alone what it took to run the club.

Earl Jackson asked where I was going and I said, "I am leaving and I'm never coming back!" Earl asked me to stay. He said to me, "Meadow, where else are you going to practice basketball? This is the only place you have to play."

This was an opportunity for me to potentially make a very bad decision. The vision of my future professional basketball career flashed before my eyes. I STAYED. I did not quit. I continued to advance my game.

If basketball hadn't worked out for me,
I might have gone Hollywood full time.

Years later, I learned one of those friends had died of a drug overdose. I was sad to hear about it. It prompted me to ask about the other friend who was with me that day. I was told I had just passed him on the street. Shocking and unrecognizable, my childhood friend was skin and bones, severely addicted to drugs and alcohol, out of his mind, and living on the streets. Not long after that, I heard he was dead.

I thought back to the day we were all going to leave the club. They never came back. It took all those years to highlight the value of a good choice. When I stayed, I not only had a place to play basketball. I also had Poppa Jack and my coaches.

An opportunity sometimes comes when you least expect it. Be ready. Life and death could be set before you at any time. Choose life.

What I *do* know is that the opportunity to play for the Globetrotters was partly fate and partly of my own creation. I had held my dream of being a Globetrotter since I was 11 and I had worked hard on my game to be the kind of player who might be good enough to be a Globetrotter.

When the opportunity came, I was prepared and I took full advantage of it.

That night eventually led to the opportunity to play with the Globetrotters in Europe, and the rest is history.

I had been blessed before with other opportunities, including some big ones I passed on! My fixation on being a Globetrotter worked out. If it hadn't, I might have been a fool who spent the next 60 years doing nothing much in Wilmington.

Thank goodness that the tryout with the Globetrotters worked out. Then Uncle Sam gave me an "opportunity," too – a draft notice into the Army.

So, as you can see, Opportunity is sometimes offered and sometimes made. And it's sometimes taken and sometimes allowed to slip away.

Before that fateful Globetrotters tryout, Marques Haynes said to me: "Young man, when you get a chance later today, make a play."

That still sounds like good advice to me. You've gotta grab an opportunity and make the most of it. You never know when the next opportunity might come. And you never know what might happen.

The Globetrotters were true to their name. We must have flown around the world dozens of times. (I'm second from the right, just behind Abe Saperstein. That is Manny Jackson fourth from the left, who was on the team from 1962-1964.)

"There is no limit to what you can accomplish if you don't care who gets the credit."

– A sign on the desk of President Ronald Reagan

"T" Means Teamwork

The **"T"** in SHOT stands for Teamwork.

This may be the most important thing of all because no one ever accomplishes anything great without teamwork. Teamwork has been defined as "joint action by two or more people."

In basketball, I was taught not to look for my shot. I was taught to make it easy for the other four players on my team to shoot and make a basket. If all five players on a team have that same mindset, everyone will get open shots and the best shooters will make easy baskets.

Every team has role players. Some players are the best at rebounding, others at defending, still others at passing. There might come a time when you'll have to take a foul for someone. Not in the illegal or immoral sense, only to protect the team. Sometimes you have to stand in there and not give up your ground.

So know what you do best in life. Recognize and understand your role, and you'll be able to make a wonderful contribution to all the winning teams in your life.

I've been on dozens and dozens of important teams in my life ...

The Globetrotters

Of course, the Globetrotters is the team for which I'm best known. Remember when we were talking about Opportunity? You'll recall that when Abe Saperstein asked me to join the Globetrotters, he was inviting me to join a TEAM.

He didn't ask me to go on tour as Meadowlark Lemon's Basketball and Comedy Show. He didn't ask me to become a star of my own, on my own.

He asked me to join a TEAM. And what a great team it was: Marques Haynes, Goose Tatum, Sweetwater Clifton, Rookie Brown, Jumping Johnny Williams, and Captain Babe Pressley.

For a while, the Globetrotters had the best player in the history of the game up to that time: Wilt "The Stilt" Chamberlain.

The players on the Globetrotters teams have changed through the years – more than 500 men have proudly worn the red-white-and blue uniform, including a wonderful one-armed player, Boid Buie out of Tennessee, and two baseball Hall-of-Famers: Bob Gibson and Ferguson Jenkins. The faces change. One thing has remained the same: it's always been a great team.

My "First Team"

My Mom, Mamie

Mom was a true New Yorker. She spent most of her life in Harlem and loved it. I tried to get her to move to Bel Air, California with me. She would always say, "I have a home." When I moved back to Arizona, she started making excuses; she would say "where would I stay?" I would tell her that she could stay with us and she would always say that there would be "too many women in the kitchen." I told her that we could get her a place three blocks down the street. We looked at a place and she liked it, and the mall was only one block away. She asked me about the public transportation. I said, "Mom, this is Arizona." After that, she said she would think about it.

In New York City, the public transportation goes all over the place. Mom would get on the bus in the morning and ride the bus all day. She would get off the bus to have coffee and meet people she knew. She loved to laugh and have a good time with her girlfriends. Mom had a very

distinct laugh that was contagious. Sometimes people would laugh just because Mom was laughing. Eventually, someone would say, "Why are we laughing?" Someone else would say, "I don't know. I'm laughing because she's laughing." I miss Mom's laugh and her smile; she could be a lot of fun!

On Sunday mornings, Mom served as an usher at her church and was president of the Usher Board for many years. She would leave home at 8 a.m. and return at 10 p.m. She and her friends would go from church to church. In almost every church there are full restaurants. You could get a big meal for just a little money. Those sisters can burn (cook)! I knew Mom needed to stay in New York where she could enjoy her friends and have the freedom to come and go whenever she pleased. She was always very independent and worked hard to keep it that way.

In the early 1960s, Mom was employed by the New York Hotel Trade Council and Association. She worked with them until her retirement. I am her only child. She called me Meadows. She would always say, "Anyone who doesn't like my son doesn't like me." Not only did Mom love me, she was proud of her only child. Every time we played at New York's Madison Square Garden, Mom would be outside the dressing room signing autographs. She would always love it when I would stand next to her and we would sign together. If Mom and I were walking down the street, she would call people over and ask them, "Do you know who this

My mom and me at Madison Square Garden outside of the dressing room – she was waiting there for me after the game so we could sign autographs together.

is?!" When we would go out to eat, she would call people over to our table and say, "This is my son, Meadowlark Lemon. Would you like an autograph?" When mom would come visit me, she always wanted to go to the airport three or four hours early, so we could walk around, meet people, and have coffee. After the 9/11 terrorist attacks she never trusted an airplane again. My Mom was Mamie. She was tough. She knew everybody and they protected her. She wasn't afraid of anyone. She would use her pocket book as a weapon. If anyone on public transportation would get too close to her or seem aggressive in any way, she would hold her pocket book up and say, "Come on sucker! I'll knock your head off." She was a pro at getting around the city on public transportation. New York City was Mom's town, the city that never sleeps.

Mom went to be with the Lord on May 15, 2004. I'm very thankful she was able to attend my enshrinement ceremony at the Naismith Memorial Basketball Hall of Fame in 2003 so that I could witness the joy on her face as she watched her only son receive the ultimate honor in the world of professional basketball. Just as I felt when Mom could attend any of my events through the years, I felt great joy knowing that my mom was proud of me. She is my mom; she is only with me in spirit now and I miss seeing her, talking to her, and hearing that beautiful laugh. Her signature is all over this book and my life. Lord God, I love my mom.

Earl "Poppa Jack" Jackson, as you know, taught me how to shoot a hook shot at the Boys' Club. Now remember, he was just a volunteer. He really had no reason to help me other than the fact that he loved kids and he saw the passion I had for basketball. I didn't know at that time, that the hook shot he taught me would become my signature play for decades with the Globetrotters.

Coach E. A. "Spike" Corbin was the assistant football coach, assistant basketball coach, and head baseball coach at Williston Industrial High School, the only black high school in Wilmington. I first played football for him, and he coaxed me to ask the head basketball coach for a chance to make the varsity team.

Well, the head basketball coach, Coach Robinson, didn't pay much attention to me at first, however, Coach Corbin kept after me to work on my game. And I eventually made the team as its center.

Coach Corbin was also the physical education and health and hygiene teacher at Williston. I learned all about anatomy from him. And I learned plenty about practicing hard and sticking to my dreams.

Long after I had been gone from Williston, Coach Corbin became the director of athletics for all of the Wilmington high schools. When I knew him, he was making 18 cents an hour. That's right: 18 cents.

I had one of the most important teammates in my life at quite a discount.

My dad, Meadow Lemon II. We already talked about the time he saved me from being run over by a car. Now that's a teammate!

Mrs. Leonard deserves a spot in my "Teammate Hall of Fame" because she insisted that I take my freshman English test before graduating from high school.

She wanted me to succeed.

That's what being a teammate is all about.

Pistol Pete

Another of my "teammates" was Peter Press Maravich, better known around basketball circles as "Pistol Pete." It was a nickname he picked up while playing for high school teams in South Carolina and North Carolina while his father, Press Maravich, coached at Clemson and North Carolina State. In both states, reporters noted that the young Maravich often shot the ball from the side of his hip, as would a gunslinger in the Old West. So, he became "Pistol Pete."

Pistol became a hit with college recruiters who were eager to bring on board the high-scoring, flashy youngster. Since Press Maravich was hired as head coach at Louisiana State University, Pete's college choice was a foregone conclusion.

Record books show a phenomenal journey for this 6' 5" guard. Twice he was selected as the United States Basketball Writers Association College Player of the Year. After averaging more than 44 points a game, he was a shoo-in to be a high pick in the NBA draft.

Just prior to the 1970 draft following his graduation from LSU, a story broke that Maravich had been offered a $1 million contract to play for the Harlem Globetrotters.

I became excited. I wondered what would happen when Pistol Pete and I teamed up. Would he bring out even more crazy antics from me on the court? Would I help to develop him into an even higher scoring threat?

Perhaps, as it had been with me and Wilt "The Stilt" Chamberlain, we would drive each other to greater heights.

I kept asking myself these questions as the team waited for Pistol Pete to make his first appearance in a Globetrotters' uniform.

After one week with Pistol still a no-show, I asked our owner, Abe Saperstein, about his arrival date.

"Won't be any," he said.

When I asked why, he told me that this whole story about Pete coming to the team was not true. It was a rumor, nothing else. "Besides," he added, "that million bucks would be 10 times what we paid for Chamberlain."

Abe's story was confirmed when Pistol Pete announced later in the week that he had turned down a huge contract with the rival American Basketball Association and was signing with the Atlanta Hawks of the NBA.

During a pro career with the Hawks, the New Orleans/Utah Jazz, and the Boston Celtics, Pistol Pete racked up nearly 16,000 points, and this was prior to the installation of a three-point shot in the NBA.

A five-time NBA All-Star selection, he was also named in 1996 as one of the 50 greatest players in the league's history.

I got to see him play several times during his illustrious career. After one of his great games, I congratulated him on his spectacular moves toward the basket.

"You should appreciate it," he responded with a huge grin on his face. "I learned it from you after watching you all these years."

A knee injury reportedly forced him into early retirement in 1980. Maravich then became a recluse for nearly two years. It was during this time of "searching" that he embraced the evangelical Christian faith.

It was the one decision that turned his life around. He proclaimed at a Billy Graham Crusade, "I want to be remembered as a Christian, a person that serves Him to the utmost, not as a basketball player."

Many times after that, Pistol Pete and I would discuss not just our mutual love for basketball, we also would talk about our kinship with the Lord.

I can testify that the Pete Maravich I got to know after his conversion to Christianity was far different from the rather wild, rambunctious, and uninhibited youngster I had known before. Now he adopted an entirely different attitude and was someone you enjoyed having around.

One time, for example, Pete had joined us for a game in Iowa during the dead of winter. Afterward, both of us stood outside the arena signing autographs for kids while snow fell and the cold wind sent chills to the bones. I was tired from the game and the freezing temperature was growing mighty uncomfortable.

After standing there for about 15 minutes, I said, "Sorry, Pete, I gotta go inside. Can't take this cold anymore."

"That's OK, Brother," he said. "I'll stay."

Sure enough, as I walked back to the arena's player entrance, I turned and saw Pete still signing autographs. I learned later that he signed them all until the last kid left.

The Pete Maravich I knew earlier would never have done that. I became convinced, based on our conversations, that it wasn't really an injury that caused Pete to leave the game. Rather, I believe, it was that he had found something in his life that was far more compelling than basketball.

It was Pete's dedication to his faith, in fact, that became one of the profound influences on my life. And it's something that I still treasure.

Although he was a dedicated Christian, Pistol Pete Maravich did not set out to become an evangelist. He didn't have time to do that. On January 5, 1988, while playing in a pickup game at a church in Pasadena, California, with a group that included James Dobson, head of the "Focus on the Family" radio and television programs, Pete collapsed and died of a heart attack.

He was only 40 years old.

Pete Maravich remains one of my heroes to this day because of his dedication to the sport of basketball and because of his even stronger devotion to his faith.

I only hope that I can maintain both of these commitments as long as I'm fortunate enough to live on this earth. Thank you, Pete, for being such a wonderful teammate to me.

It Takes a Village

You know the saying, "It takes a village?" I think that's true. It takes a lot of people to help show a young person the way. We might like to believe that every child has strong parents in their life who can teach them proper values and lasting virtues. Unfortunately, that's just not so. Some children need caring adults from outside the family – teachers, mentors, ministers, neighbors, friends.

I like to think of all those people as not just a "village." They are also our community "teammates."

Just like in basketball, it's the duty of teammates to pass on love and guidance, to make sure children practice right with their studies, and to lift them up if they get knocked to the floor during the game of life.

So don't be afraid to gently say something to a group of kids who might be out doing something they shouldn't be doing. Agree to be a mentor to a kid at your church.

Sign up for the Big Brothers program. Become a leader in your village. Pay back those older people who were there for you.

Meadowlark Lemon Ministries and My Outreach Teams

My life as a basketball celebrity has been no accident. As one of the world's most recognizable athletes and entertainers, I have access to millions who might not otherwise hear the Good News. God has used my past to open a door to others' futures. In 1986, I became an ordained minister, and in 1998, I received a Doctorate of Divinity from Vision

International University. I have created many outreach teams over the past years and proudly serve with the likes of Mercy Ministries, Muhammad Ali's Celebrity Fight Night, Trinity Broadcasting Network, Daystar, Smile of a Child Foundation, Starkey Hearing Foundation-So the World May Hear, Lenny Wilkins Foundation, Albert Pujol's Foundation, and foundations established by David Robinson, Michael Jordan, Walter Payton, Fergie Jenkins, Bobby Mitchell, Boys and Girls Clubs, Salvation Army, groups that raise money for police and firemen, and so many more.

With the Globetrotters, God blessed me with a wonderful opportunity and the skills to make the most of it. Then God blessed me a second time. I get to be a part of an even greater team; a team with a heart for people and a mission for the world; a team with a message of hope and redemption. That team is the Meadowlark Lemon Ministries, and it's been my most important team for over 20 years. We are committed to support the ministries and organizations that serve local communities and citizens in almost every city in the United States and some internationally. My message is that the most meaningless statistic in life is the half-time score – and the choices we make today count.

"I have seen basketball players score 40 points a game and their team still lose. If that same player will score 20 points and learn to pass the ball and be part of a team, that team wins games!" – Meadowlark Lemon

Camp Meadowlark

Camp Meadowlark is a specially created basketball camp designed to improve young people's basketball skills while also teaching them the importance of education and staying healthy. It is a complete program to teach youngsters the important skills and fundamentals of basketball.

We emphasize four attributes of basketball: physical, psychological, social, and spiritual. Physical conditioning is a key factor in the longevity of my career, and the difference between an average player and one of the legends of the game. I teach them about applying the mental or psychological parts of the game to everyday life to handle pressure, to set goals, and to strengthen moral character. Socially, we need to be able to interact with players and individuals from all other walks of life, regardless of gender, race, color or creed. I train these kids spiritually to give God the glory for all our talents and gifts.

I am personally dedicated to every camper. Our kids are 100% of our future! It's a unique and fun-filled learning experience with a focus on becoming a total player. I teach them to learn the skills, when to use them, how to practice, then put them to use. These are the fundamentals upon which I built a career. As a special feature, these kids get passing, dribbling, and basketball-handling skills. These camps are especially effective in the inner-city, as well as anywhere we can fit a couple of hundred kids with some basketball goals.

Youth Drug Awareness Program

I remember being that young child playing basketball on a sandlot in the "neighborhood." There were lots of other things I could have spent my time doing that were not healthy. Fast forward a few years, and some of the same kids I spent time with died of drug overdoses and their lives were snuffed out prematurely. Drugs start by taking out one person, which will take out a family, then a whole block can go. We need fathers back in our inner-city neighborhoods. In the same way, we take our neighborhoods back one person at a time.

I have been actively helping young people avoid the catastrophe of drug abuse alongside Les "Pee Wee" Harrison and Tyrone "Hollywood" Brown. We use our basketball talents to break down barriers and prepare each message with the guidance of the

Supporting a variety of charities is important to me. Here I am with actor Robert Stack at a charity event.

local school systems. We also incorporate the support of local anti-alcohol and drug-abuse agencies, as well as local police. Or aim is to build trust, understanding, and a positive self-image among students as a fortress against the devastation of drug abuse.

Youth Prison Work

We have a special heart for young people in prison. We feel that God has anointed us to help these troubled youngsters so that they can see and experience the love of Jesus Christ. Our hope and intention is that they will never reach adult prisons. At a youth prison in Washington where we recently ministered, nearly all of the prisoners gave their hearts to the Lord.

I was originally moved to get involved in youth prison work when I heard the story of a 9-year-old boy who had been imprisoned 32 times because there was no place else for him to go.

We have a responsibility to the youth to begin to help them. Everything is out of hand now because we took prayer and God out of the schools. I do ministry in prisons simply because I believe we change the future one child at a time. It's as simple as that.

The kids in the penal system want to be bad and tough, even though they still have baby faces. I believe we have a duty to look out for our youth and train them up in the way they should go.

Ministry to the Native Americans

God has placed a dream upon the heart of my family and I to bring love and hope to the nations first people, the Indian Nations on our forgotten lands. Meadowlark Lemon Ministries, Inc. and Meadowlark Lemon's Harlem All Stars™ have partnered with Pastors Ray and Ceci Ramos of the Festival of Life World Outreach Ministries from the United Auburn Indian Community in Auburn, California. While we have been working with the Native American community for many years, the last several years we have worked closely with our friends, Pastors Ray and Ceci. Other ministries are reaching out to Native Americans. We believe that the Meadowlark name and reputation have allowed us to minister to many groups who might be difficult for others to reach. For example, we have access to several Native American reservations in Arizona and California. There, we help raise funds with comedic basketball games while bringing the Good News of the gospel to the people. We are now planning a series of Camp Meadowlark Basketball Camps for the reservations, which are often very poor in facilities and resources.

Pastor Ceci is a beautiful American Indian from the Miwok tribe, with the gift of giving and bringing joy to others. Pastor Ceci prefers to be called American Indian. Pastor Ray has great insight from the Word of God and teaches how to live in prosperity and God's blessings. The entire Ramos family has been bringing joy to many Indian reservations for years, as well as to anyone who is fortunate enough to be blessed by their presence and their efforts. Our ministry, working with theirs, hopes to provide compassionate, loving, and competent services in the name of Christ to a forgotten people. These beautiful Indian people are struggling to live through some of the most rugged conditions that exist, while trying to maintain a sense of self worth. Their environment can be harsh and oppressive. We are developing programs to provide medicine, toiletries, water, coats, blankets, food and other essential goods.

Evangelism is at the heart of all we do. Our most important mission is to provide spiritual help and life-changing principles by proclaiming the Good News! We accomplish this by demonstrating Christ's love through our relief efforts. We also promote native leadership and training native ministry leaders.

I have the greatest respect for the many Native American pastors who I have worked alongside. They face difficult life issues, work long hours, and many have to hold down full-time jobs just to continue in ministry. Many times we're quick to think we have it bad and then we look around and see that there are others who also face tremendous struggles and hardships. I often tell Ray and Ceci that one of my dreams for the Native American people is to motivate Native American athletes to reach professional status.

Leadership by Example, Service with Honor

Finally, I try to lead spiritually by filling in as a chaplain for the NBA, and the NFL to support my fellow athletes who are role models to this generation. I encourage and support our troops at the military academy's and bases across the country and abroad. I remember my drill sergeants well, and my fellow soldiers are always in my heart - the Army, Navy, Air Force, and Marines, Reserves and Coast Guard. We all would do well to honor our servicemen and women as often as possible.

My Hall of Fame Team

One of the most prestigious teams I'm on is at the Naismith Memorial Basketball Hall of Fame. I won the Hall's John W. Bunn Lifetime Achievement Award in 2000. That award is the Hall's highest honor outside of actual induction.

I was included when the Harlem Globetrotters were inducted as a team in 2002. I was individually enshrined as a contributor to the international game of basketball in 2003.

I am humbled and proud to be on the hall's legendary team, with about 300 other basketball immortals.

Here's what I had to say about what induction meant to me – my actual speech from the enshrinement ceremony. Mannie Jackson, my dear, dear friend, introduced me.

Mannie Jackson, executive with the Harlem Globetrotters and a former player with the team, introduced Meadowlark Lemon at his induction into the Naismith Memorial Basketball Hall of Fame in Springfield, Massachusetts, in 2003.

"You know, induction into the Hall of Fame is a major life milestone for the inductee. However, there are a few instances where the induction is also a

milestone for the Hall of Fame. It's an important part of its foundation and future credibility. I'm honored tonight to introduce a case in point. This gentleman is, in fact, an American legend.

This is my 10th year of owning the Harlem Globetrotters. And the longer I'm around, the more amazed I am at the many accomplishments and the magnitude of the love the world has for Meadowlark Lemon. I remind you that he was not a made-for-television celebrity pushed upon us by cola manufacturers or shoe marketers. To millions of fans around the world, he is the original, live Showtime. No station breaks, no reruns, no edited highlight films, just Meadowlark. Up close and very personal, Globetrotter style.

His playing days date back to a time when segregation in sports was the norm. And a society separated by race was a constant reminder of a flawed society. But like few others, he was undaunted. He was proud. I knew him to be talented, smart, funny, and simply irresistible. He believed if you accepted him first on the basis of his many talents and his integrity, and if he could make someone laugh, he would get you to listen, to believe, and to change. He did just that for 24 years. He changed people's attitudes about race. He changed foreigners' attitudes about America. And along the way, he made millions love the game of basketball.

Tonight's enshrinement, as I said before, marks the fourth time we've been up here. We've received the coveted John W. Bunn Lifetime Award. Meadowlark received that last year. The Harlem Globetrotters as a team was introduced last year. Today, we introduce the Clown Prince. One of the best basketball players that ever lived.

Tonight is a deserving tribute for Meadowlark. He joins former teammates Marques Haynes, who's here tonight, Wilt Chamberlain, and Pop Gates. This will surprise you: He played in over 7,500 consecutive games, in approximately

100 countries. Still, as legend has it, he missed one game in 24 years. And I know he's known around the world as a master comic, but those of us who played with him knew him as an unusually gifted athlete. Off the court, I knew him as a serious speaker, an analyst, a deep thinker, a gentle-but-strong man and a thoughtful human being who always cared deeply about what he was and what had been given to him.

Today, he has transferred his love of God to a global ministry. He's a family man and a father of 10 who dotes on his wife, Cynthia, and his son, Caleb. He had zero tolerance for mediocrity and absolute disdain for anyone who didn't respect the 24/7 preparation and performance standards of being a professional athlete, and a Harlem Globetrotter. Because you see for Meadowlark, being a Globetrotter wasn't a job, this was his calling. His business was playing basketball at the highest level and making people feel good, while creating positive, lasting memories.

Meadowlark may not have been the best movie actor, the best recording artist, the best TV sitcom star, the best coach and maybe not the best minister. Or cattle rancher. Or sports team owner. But he holds two undeniable leadership positions in the history of sports. First, he is the undisputed global leader and champion at being loved and remembered by fans all over the world. And no one will ever touch the hearts of families and young people in the way that he has. Secondly, I cannot believe the deadly accurate, crazy half-court hook shot of his. I have watched him do it a thousand times and it simply defies the laws of physics.

Boys and girls, ladies and gentlemen, sports fans everywhere, I introduce Hall-of-Famer, my friend and a gentleman I've called an angel: The good reverend, Meadowlark Lemon."

This is my enshrinement speech

Thank you. Hallelujah. That means that I love you. And tonight I'm happy. I'm happy to be here. Thank you so much for
all of the kind words, and hopefully I can give a little something
back, even before this is all over. Man, I've had a good run. I've
had a great run. It's been wonderful. It's time to light up. It's time
to light up. This is it.

When I was 11 years old, I used to go to the Ritz Theater every
Saturday morning at 10 o'clock. And we had to be back home at
8:00. And my daddy didn't mean one minute past 8:00. He didn't
know anything about child abuse, OK? So I would leave the Ritz
Theater at two minutes to 8:00, so I could be back on time.

In the Ritz Theater we would watch five cartoons, three
westerns, and anything else they put on there. We saw the Green
Hornet sometimes. We saw Batman without Robin. And then
we got the newsreel because in those days we didn't have television; if you had television you were rich and nobody in my block
was rich, so we didn't have any television. We got the news from
the newsreel every Saturday morning and we would stay in the
Ritz Theater and watch it over and over. My dad would give me
enough money to buy a piece of Washington pie, which was old

bread puddin' – not bread pudding, bread puddin', you see there's a difference to it. It was real heavy and when you mixed that RC Cola with it, something supernatural would happen way down inside.

And I could stay in the Ritz Theater all day long and watch the runs all over and over again. But this one day I saw this basketball team. You see, in my neighborhood, we didn't play basketball because we said it was a no-touch sport, so we wanted to play touch sports. We played baseball. We didn't throw the ball across the plate, we threw it at each other. We played football in the streets. There were no out-of-bounds, you could run all around the house, it didn't matter. But this particular day, I saw these men in the dressing room, and they were singing, they were playing their music and they were putting their sneakers – no, they were tennis shoes, we didn't have sneakers – they were tennis shoes. They were not pumps; they didn't cost $150 and we still made out all right. But they were putting these shoes on and they walked to the basketball court and when they got to the basketball court, they seemed to make that ball talk. I said, "That's mine. This is for me." I was receiving a vision. I was receiving a dream in my heart.

I left the Ritz Theater early that day to get home so that I could learn how to play basketball and when I got home I didn't have any place to play. I made my own hoop out of a coat hanger and an onion sack and I nailed it up across the street on a tree. And there was a big iron pipe out there. For my basketball I had a Carnation milk can. And I'd grab that pole and I'd swing around and I'd learn how to shoot that hook shot. I'd be out there every day until they let me into the Boys Club. The Boys and Girls Club of Wilmington, North Carolina. That hook shot. (Cliff) Hagan, where are you? Oh, you had a smooth hook shot, man. Kareem (Abdul-Jabbar), oh man, you did it. You did it. Those are the three hook shots I've known in my life. Hagan, Kareem and Meadow-lark's hook shot with a lot of lemon flavor on it.

I have a lot of people that I have to apologize to, and I don't want to leave anything undone. A lot of people I need to apologize to. Those people I've hurt in any way in my lifetime I apologize tonight. I ask their forgiveness. George, my son, we did a program for one of the networks and he cried. He said, "My dad was gone so much we missed something. We missed him." Robin, my daughter – one of my daughters here tonight – she missed her dad because I was on the road playing basketball. And we decided to play basketball because we felt that we could give the kids a better education because I could make just a little more money out there and we stayed on the road. Donna and Robin, George, Beverly, John. I apologize to y'all tonight. Derek, you suffered the most. I didn't get a chance to spend any time with you. I apologize for that. Mom, I love you and I apologize to you because I haven't spent time with you. Crystal, Caleb … these are tears of joy. It's not an act – I'm not that good. Jamison, Angela, my life has been chapter after chapter, this is the middle of the book and you're going to get the best of me with my wife, Cynthia, you're going to get the best of the book. You're right in the middle because I'm going to be around a long, long time.

My friends who came here from California, Arizona, and those of you who came from other states, thank you so much for being here. Mannie and I, we … someone said that we couldn't play basketball, we were clowns, and one year we got in the car when we had a couple of months off and we traveled across the state to show people, hey we can get down. And it felt good. But little did we know that everybody knew we could play.

Jerry Saperstein, my friend ... and his son, his only son, he came to be with me tonight. We grew up on the bus. And I love your dad, man. He hooked this thing up. This man came out of baseball and found some guys playing in the sandlot. He called them the Chicago Savoy Five and he began to hook this thing up. And that's where we are today.

There's just so many other people out there today, all the players: Curly Neal, Geese, the Hawk, the Big Dipper. You know, there's people in our lives that made all this happen. It just didn't happen. Somebody threw the ball to you. Mr. Haynes, thank you, sir. You gave me the first shot. And there've been so many other people. I'm sorry that I've forgotten some of the names of the people that I want to talk about tonight. Man, but it's been great. I mean it's been great. I've had a wonderful time and the best is yet to come. I'm 16 games shy of playing 16,000. I'm 75 games shy of playing in 10,000 consecutives. It's gonna happen, y'all. Someone said, well how can you do that? You're too old. If you're not too old to watch, we can handle it.

Write your vision and make it plain upon tables, that he may run that readeth it. For the vision is yet for an appointed time, but at the end it shall speak, and not lie: though it tarry, wait for it. Your vision will surely come to pass. I can guarantee it. Your vision will surely come to pass. I'm talking to some of you young athletes out there right now. These Hall-of-Famers sitting in this room tonight have made it possible for you to do what you're doing. When they ask us, aren't you sorry you didn't come along to make the big dollars? If we don't make what we did, if we don't do what we did, if we don't ride the bus all those many miles, if Bill Russell – I see Jerry West over here – if he didn't play as hard as he played out there. Cous (Bob Cousy), I don't see you, man, but you were out there doing it. You were making it all happen. Earl Lloyd. You young kids think that you can jump today? He was doing it 50 years ago. Y'all ought to take note: to K.C. (Jones) over here, how he played defense.

If you want to fulfill the vision, you'll write it down. My time is up. They're giving me this sign that means give it up. But that's OK. I've said all I can say, anyway. One of the young men in one of my basketball camps, he came up to me one day and said, "Mr. Meadowlark?" I said, "Yeah?" He said, "You've got it going on." Well tonight, we have it going on.

"Meadowlark Lemon is an American institution whose uniform should hang alongside the Spirit of St. Louis and the Gemini Space Capsule in the halls of the Smithsonian Institute."

- Los Angeles Times sportswriter Jim Murray

My Team Today

The team I have with me today is the best of my life. Cynthia is my wife of 17 years. She is a doctor of naturopathy and has a Ph.D. in nutritional philosophy. She has me on a program that keeps me feeling strong and healthy. I love my 10 kids and all my 15 grandchildren.

Cynthia and I are a team. Not a 50%-50% team, a 100%-100% team! Separate people who operate as one effective unit. She's my pretty side!

We have been working together for 17 years and counting. We know each other better than anyone. In cultivating our ministry, foundation, and basketball team, and in managing a household and parenting many children, there are some areas where she is stronger than I am and there are things at which I'm stronger than she. Put it all together and it's teamwork!

Together, we are winners. We look out for each other. She is a blessing to me. She looks for ways to make my day easier and better. It was no accident that we met where we met and when we met – at church.

This was in God's plan for us and for our children, and for the child we had together, Caleb Lark Lemon, who was born on September 11, 1994.

Cynthia needed a man she could count on, who kept his word, and with whom she felt safe. I am that man for her. I needed a woman I could trust. I found a true, faithful friend and partner.

She is the steward of all I do. I am the face of the ministry that everyone sees, and she is the body or pillar that holds me up. I appreciate that.

She sees me as a man first, then as a professional athlete and a public figure. I see her as my woman, and then as a doctor who has helped countless people regain their health and strength.

After we married, the athletes with whom I train with began to tell me how I was looking younger and stronger than I had in years. So I'm one of her patient success stories myself.

We appreciate our differences. We have been able to blend our families and ministries into one. She has not only been able to develop a ministry of health, she also has been a great blessing to ensure my health and longevity. We believe our health is both spiritual and physical.

Here's one of my favorites stories in my whole life – the story of how Cynthia and I met:

I was a guest speaker at my home church in Scottsdale, Arizona. It was 1993. I'd been attending church every chance I got when I wasn't on the road ministering or playing basketball somewhere. Our pastor, Michael Maiden, you could tell he'd spent a lot of time with God and was teaching us the truth of God's word. I liked to study the Bible in the same way that I studied basketball. He was teaching me the fundamental truth of God's word.

So I'm the guest speaker. I'm a single professional basketball player talking to the singles group on a Friday night. Someone told me there were more female attendees that night than the usual singles gatherings would typically draw in. Praise the Lord, I thought. These singles must really love Jesus!

I was telling them how I'd been single. How I'd been married. How I was single now. I never had any challenges with drugs or alcohol. Women, well, that was different.

I'd admired families for years, and had been unable to cultivate the type of home life I truly wanted for myself and my children. So I'm telling the singles group how the money, the fame, and the women did not satisfy me. There was an emptiness in my heart. The King of Kings, Jesus Christ, is the one who gave any real meaning to anything in my past or what looked like my future.

This was good stuff! I'm pouring my heart out for these folks. I'm praying they would learn from my life lessons, and avoid some of the heartaches I had experienced. I asked if anyone would like to meet this Jesus, to come down front and I would introduce them. It would be simple, and he would do the same for them that he had done for me.

So why were three ladies laughing during my altar call? They were having a great time, making all kinds of noise. I like a good joke as much as the next guy. I wondered what they were laughing about. I finished praying up front, and oozed over to the row of ladies in question. Since they were no longer paying me any mind, I got to startle them quite nicely. "What seems to be so funny, ladies?"

"Oh, we are so sorry, Mr. Lemon. We did not mean to interrupt your prayer time." Her voice was like honey. I like how she called me Mr. Lemon. I didn't know at that time that she was to be my future wife. I had seen her walking toward me a few Sundays back. She looked good walking that direction. As she passed me by, she looked just as good walking away. That was good walking.

"You see these two," she said, pointing to her daughter, Angela, and Angela's grandmother, Naomi Stout, both of whom were seated next to her. "They had a really tough day together. They just worked it out."

I smiled. Laughter and overcoming challenges has been part of my story from day one. We chatted for a few minutes. I wanted to see her again.

I married her three months later. Exactly. It's like the Lord to put a desire in a heart, and then make the puzzle pieces fit. We don't have to know everything all at once. Just know he puts treasures around you, in your path every day and look forward to finding them.

Her name was Cynthia. Everyone called her Cindy. (Not me, I like Cynthia.) She had three children, a boy and two girls. I like kids. I have six of my own, I tell her eventually. That night of the singles meeting, I found out later, Cynthia had wanted to give me her business card and let me know she would be willing to use her training as a naturopathic doctor to assist my ministry when we worked with at-risk youth. However, she had quickly changed her mind and returned the card to her jacket pocket when she felt approaching me at a singles meeting and giving me her contact information may give me the wrong impression of her intentions. She whispered a quiet prayer, "Lord, if you want Meadowlark to have this business card let him come to me and get it himself." Not minutes later, I was there.

Our first meal together (I call it a date), she let me know that she had never seen me play basketball, although she had heard I wasn't too bad. I wondered what planet she was from. So I asked her, "What planet are you from?" We laughed. She said, "I remember my dad, who loved basketball, especially loved watching the Globetrotters on TV. Now I wish I would have watched the games with him." Well, I could deal with that. I ordered the lobster. She told me they were not good for me. I changed my order to the soft shell crab. Um, not those, either. "O-kaaaay. How about I have what you are having?" We have salmon. She has no idea about basketball. Or any sports. Really? I would have to teach her a thing or two.

To this day, while I'm sure she still appreciates my legendary status, I still need to take our family's trash out. I may be famous, however I still have to know where the garbage goes. After we were married, she moved in to my house in Scottsdale and brought me a son, Jamison (18), a daughter, Angela (17), and a delightful five-year-old girl named Crystal Joy. They made that house a home. I still love coming off the road and walking in the door and being greeted by my family. The following year, the whole lot of us celebrated the birth of our son, Caleb Lark Lemon. Ten children – we could take the Brady Bunch if we wanted to. We have them outnumbered.

That's me and Cynthia with our son, Caleb Lark Lemon, at a celebrity fund-raising event.

We blended our family sitting around the kitchen table. I prepared communion with grape juice and crackers and blessed them. I read to them about how God the Father accepts us through Jesus Christ. I told them I accepted them as my children, and because I got to choose them they were special to me. They listened and didn't say much. Over the years, it has been a fundamental building block of our blended family. The Holy Spirit has taught me to be a better father. I didn't have the opportunity to be home with my older children for extended periods of time. If it could be done over, I would love to have spent more quality time with them when they were small. Their mother and I decided all those years ago we were going to make the sacrifice and I would join the Harlem Globetrotters and play basketball to ensure the children would be well-educated and provided for. I wasn't perfect then or now, and I've learned to be grateful and appreciative of every moment with each of them. God the Father is perfect, and His example gives me the fundamentals and wisdom I need to cultivate a rich family life. I didn't have that ability before I met Jesus Christ. Before, I was able to be a good provider, and now I can be both. My 10 kids are every color of the rainbow. They give me joy! Each one is a unique expression of my life.

My world had a few new challenges for them, too. Cynthia told HBO (the entire cable network!) when asked by an interviewer, "What makes Meadowlark a great husband?" She quickly answered, "He's a great husband because he's a great friend, a great lover, a great father and provider to our children." I should have taught her a thing or two about the editing of pre-taped interviews. As far as anyone knows now, after editing the shoot, my wife thinks I'm a great husband because I'm a great lover. That's it. Hey, now! At least she didn't marry me for my money! And here's another thing I can kid her about. Her mom told me that she and her husband had taken Cynthia to see me and the Globetrotters in Indiana when Cynthia was two or three years old. (I must have made a subconscious impression on her at that game!)

Cynthia and I are partners; teammates in marriage, parenting, and ministry. We own and operate The Meadowlark Lemon Foundation, Meadowlark Lemon Ministries, Inc., and Meadowlark Lemon's Harlem All Stars. We are a team. We build the values of our home together: honor, respect, integrity, responsibility, forgiveness. The values of your family "team" will flow out from your home all over the world through your children. It is a daily choice to decide to be in agreement, a choice to forgive and respect. At first it can be work, and it feels clumsy, not unlike me trying to throw that milk can through an onion sack. Eventually though, the reaction is cellular. Your body and mind remember it. You begin to do it automatically. You will begin to forgive others even before you have time to be angry.

My wife and I had each dealt with major betrayals and hurts in our past. We had both made mistakes. Together, by the grace and mercy of God, we are made new. The Bible says, "His mercies are new every morning." He has short, 24-hour accounts with us. It's true what they say – "Don't go to bed angry." God has provided us with new wisdom for those old challenges and he keeps working it out for us. I see His handy work every day.

Love notes from my children.
I am truly blessed

Son: Richard Derrick Battle – New York, N.Y.

"I am my father's first son. My parents were so young when I was born. I was adopted and raised in a loving home. God had a plan that was best. I have come to understand who and what my father is to me and society at large from a distance. I applaud him, my biological father, who brought great joy to people all over the world … the legend, the name, the ambassador, the sportsman, is undeniable."

Son: Meadow George Lemon – Portland, Oregon

"How appropriate that my father would write a book pertaining to joy. My father is a man who has spent a lifetime spreading joy throughout the world. So many of Dad's fans have personally shared with me their gratitude for the joy and memories he brought to them over the years. I now understand exactly what it is that his fans through the years have been sharing with me. It's pure joy when I see my dad's eyes light up when he sees his grandkids, and it reminds me of the same heartfelt joy I felt in the days when I used to sit next to him on the bench during the hey-days of the Globetrotters. My dad should be inducted into the Hall of Fame of Joy!"

Daughter: Beverly Lemon – Berwyn, Pennsylvania

"I work for the United States Navy. Growing up with a famous father, we didn't realize he was famous; we only knew he was Dad and we loved him. In the first grade, when asked what our fathers did for a living, I announced proudly my father is a dishwasher. I had seen him in the kitchen the night before washing dishes, although my teacher knew he was a Globetrotter. My father made history with the Globetrotters and opened doors for a new generation of athletes. We are all proud of Dad and we'll always be a family."

Daughter: Donna Lemon-Sullivan – Berwyn, Pennsylvania

"Sitting at courtside and watching my dad work was not only fun, it was family time. He and my mom saw to that. Just a wink from his wonderful eyes, or an air-blown kiss, or his signature smile – all the while entertaining the fans – and I knew with a surety that my dad loved our family."

Daughter: Lieutenant Commander (US Navy) Robin Lemon-Soape – Washington, DC

"Reflecting on my years growing up, I had no concept of my dad being a famous celebrity. My dad's employment was not the focus. Even seeing him on television did not make me think my dad was a celebrity. I used to say, "That is just his job."

I remember coming out of Madison Square Garden, and the fans were yelling, "Mead'lark, can I get your autograph on my program? Mead'lark,

Mead'lark, we love you."

The Globetrotters had such an aggressive and extensive schedule, like no other team in the world. They played nine months in the U.S. and three months overseas. The schedule was on the refrigerator door. I remember the extraordinary gifts my sisters and I would receive when Dad came off the road. I also remember answering the phone when the State Department (Mr. Henry Kissinger's office) called to speak with my dad as they were preparing for their three-month European tour.

I began to understand the impact my dad had on the world when my sister and I were foreign exchange students in France. My host family, speaking to us in French, stated they knew my dad.

Now I understand the greater impact my dad has had on the world. I am a Lieutenant Commander of the United States Navy and I travel to different nations around the world. I do not go to a country or nation of the world where the people have not been touched by my dad. I realize the gift of joy and laughter and healing was all a part of God's plan."

Son: Jonathan Lemon – Florida

"We all love Dad and are very proud of him. I've given him two beautiful grandkids to be proud of. My son, Gabriel, has recently joined the Navy and my daughter, Zoe, is just finishing high school."

Son: Jamison Fairfield – St. Petersburg, Florida

"Dad taught me about tough love and he has been the most positive male role model for me in my life and family. He loves our large diverse

family. We don't get to see each other very often. When we think Meadowlark (or for the grandkids, Poppy), a smile always comes to mind. He takes good care of Mom and my family and for that, he is good with me. I thank him for his prayers and his advice."

Daughter: Angela Fairfield – Scottsdale, Arizona

"You adopted my brother and sister and I by your own free choice. I thank you for doting on my mom and showing her what a man of God really looks like. I'm glad for your patience with me until I understood what you meant when you told us: "Today I became your father, and

 you are my children." You opened the door for so much experience and opportunity in my life. It was overwhelming at first. You have become my peace, my friend, my counselor, my mentor, and my daddy. Your very presence in a room calls a person to a greater level of commitment to their task at hand. I am humbled by your hard work and commitment to expect more out of yourself than anyone else ever could. One of my greatest treasures besides having a mom who is amazing, and whose life taught me that God answers prayers, is having a dad who decided on his own to be there for me, and remained constant and strong while I figured out just how awesome that is."

Daughter: Crystal Joy Lemon – Scottsdale, Arizona

"Living life as a Lemon is something that I will always be thankful for, especially because I was not born a Lemon. I was chosen to be a Lemon. From the day that Mom and Meadowlark married, Angela, Jamison, and I were his children and that was it. We were flesh and blood. He was our dad. I remember when I was about 9 or 10, and another kid told me that Dad was just our "Step-Dad" and that did not count. I was very hurt by those words, and I immediately went to go tell Mom and Dad about it. Before I could even finish the story, Dad told me, "Sweetheart, you are my child no matter what anyone says." His love and his dedication to his family, no matter what happens … we always know he will be there for us. He gives me daily inspiration. He is a father I not only love, but also respect and admire. To me, my parents are my heroes. Dad and Mom always taught us through their words and, most importantly, through their actions, to be people of faith, to judge others by the content of their character and not by the color of their skin, to work hard, and that knowing the fundamentals and practicing them doesn't just apply to the basketball court – it applies to your life."

From Me, Meadowlark, with love:

Son: Caleb Lark Lemon

To my youngest child, Caleb Lark Lemon, who's only 15 years old as this book is being written: I see your many interests in basketball and hockey and in filmmaking and acting. I'm looking forward to your bright future.

(To Dad: "I love you and I'm thankful and grateful that you're my Dad." Love, Caleb)

Like I said ... I am truly blessed ... To all of my 10 children and to my 15 grandchildren and four great-grandchildren so far, you are dearly loved. You are each a gift to me, and also to the world. You're 100% of our future.

Here's Caleb in his basketball uniform. Notice his hands: he has his dad's long fingers.

Caralee J. Hursey

To my only living parent, my mother-in-law: Caralee J. Hursey and my two brothers-in-law and their families: Clint and Tim Hursey, I'm thankful for my team there in Indiana. You are my mom and my brothers and we are connected for life.

In addition to my wife and family, I am thankful for Dr. Jerry Savelle, in Fort Worth, Texas. He is a spiritual father to me. When I first became a Christian, he taught me more in an hour than most men learn in a lifetime. He had been praying for my salvation for many years. He taught me love. I'm thankful for his guidance and mentoring and his friendship.

I am thankful for my pastor and friend, Dr. Michael Maiden at Church for the Nations in Phoenix. Pastor Maiden's influence on my life has been so valuable over these last 20 years. He is a spiritual father to me, also. Not only did I meet my wife at this church, we were married in our pastor's home. My family cherishes the Maidens and we honor them for the commitment they've made as a family to minister the joy of the Lord to the nations.

I am blessed by the ministry and the friendship of Pastors Ray and Ceci Ramos in Auburn, California, Dr. Fred Price out in Los Angeles, and Dr. Alan Granger in New Mexico. You all are part of my spiritual team, and a rich blessing to me personally. Everything I've learned from you I bring with me to the world.

So, dear reader, that's my team. What about yours? On paper, write down the names of those closest to you that are on your team. List why they are important to you. Pick up the phone, send them an e-mail. Be thankful for their love and support, now, each day, and forever.

"How far you go in life depends on your being tender with the young, compassionate with the aged, sympathetic with the striving, and tolerant of the weak and strong. Because someday in your life you will have been all of these."

– George Washington Carver

Chapter 15

Assists

I have always believed that helping others is the best way to help yourself. Nothing gives me more joy than helping someone – one person or a whole crowd of people – have a better day or a better view of their life. In those instances where I've led someone to God, or maybe I should say back to God, I've felt a deep sense of satisfaction and joy.

I love to help. I love to pass out "assists."

In basketball, an assist is when one player passes the ball to another player in such a way that the second player is directly able to score a basket. An assist is especially good if the first player had a chance to shoot the ball himself, but passed it to another player who had a better shot, a better opportunity to put the ball in the hoop. Great assists are cheered just as loudly as great shots. They are a symbol of unselfishness and team play.

John Stockton, the amazing point guard for the Utah Jazz all those years, retired with the NBA's record for assists – 15,806 in his career! Can you believe that? Almost 16,000 times, he helped a teammate score a basket. That's selfless playing. That's playing team ball with a capital "T."

Oscar "Big O" Robertson is regarded as one of the greatest players in NBA history. He was an extremely versatile player, and if his first five seasons are taken together, he averaged a triple-double over those 400-plus games, with an incredible 30.3 points, 10.4 rebounds, and 10.6 assists. For his career, Robertson had 181 triple-doubles, a record that has never been approached. This was all before the existence of a 3-point shot. That's a team player.

Wayne Gretzky, whose nickname was "The Great One," holds the National Hockey League record for assists in his career with 1,963. The interesting thing about assists in hockey is that a lot of times more than one player assists on the same goal. Sometimes, two or three players get credit for an assist on the same goal. That's a great example of team play.

We should all try to be like Stockton and Gretzky, looking to help someone else make a score. Better yet, be like "Big O," who did things no one else has ever done with his ability to assist, rebound, and score.

Think about all the people who have assisted you in your life. Your parents probably helped you get started, even if their best help was to get you here on the planet. You may have gotten an assist from your grandparents and maybe from some aunts and uncles. If you have ever played organized sports, you got an assist from coaches who tried to make you a better player in whatever sport you were involved with. Teachers gave you all kinds of assistance!

You've had assists from all kinds of friends and business associates through the years. You might have gotten help from a counselor, a minister, or a mentor. Nobody gets too far without some kind of help, no matter how independent and self-reliant you believe you are.

So, now I'm asking you to give back. If you can, give back to those same people who have helped you. If they have passed on or have simply fallen out of your life, look for others to assist.

Small acts of kindness make a huge difference. A kind word, encouragement, a smile, taking time to listen, putting someone in touch with another person you know could help. How about a prayer or a blessing?

Every person is important and created by God. If you are alive, you have a purpose to be here – an assignment from God. If all that works on your body is your mouth, you can still give someone a kind word and a smile.

If you plant joy, you get joy.
- Meadowlark Lemon

We should perform kindnesses for children, especially. They are like seeds. If you plant evil, you get evil. If you plant love, you get love. If you plant joy, you get joy. A kindness toward a child is like watering a seed.

If you have the ability to do it, you can help others who might need an assist with money or other resources. I take this one very seriously. Remember the saying, "To whom much has been given, much is expected." I feel I've been given a lot, and through my ministries, I give back as much as I can.

I am reminded of one game early in my days with the Globetrotters when I had a fantastic night, scoring, passing, getting lots of laughs. I looked at our road manager, Duckie Moore, expecting that he might give me a word of praise. He looked at me and said something I will never forget: "Mead-eo, all you did was your job." He was right. I knew from that moment on that you have to do more than just your job if you possibly can.

There are thousands of ways to help. The key is to look for opportunities. You don't always have to shoot – sometimes, it's all about the assist!

A prayer can be like a beautiful assist in basketball. It can really help a "teammate."

No Intentional Fouls

In basketball, sometimes it is a winning strategy to intentionally foul one of the other team's players. Hit down on their arms as they are trying to shoot or grab them around the waist as they are driving the lane.

Maybe you're trying to save a few precious ticks of the clock and need to get the ball back near the end of a close game. Or maybe a player is going in for an easy bucket, so you foul him and make him earn his two points from the free throw line.

Intentional fouls are an accepted part of the game.

In life, we should never commit an intentional foul. We should never do hurtful things on purpose. Don't ever try to get "even" or "make someone pay." Plenty of accidental fouls are going to happen, so don't add to them by doing intentional harm to people and relationships.

Meekness, which is one of the holy virtues, is when you have the power and strength to do harm and yet you choose not to. Showing restraint is true power. Uncontrolled power and lack of restraint can cause much more harm than good.

There is power in forgiveness when someone "fouls" you. I've learned to live a life of forgiveness, including forgiving myself. We all are doing the best we can with the information we have at the time. We learn from our mistakes and challenges and do better the next time the situation presents itself.

Everything in my life has not been peaches and cream. You might try being on the road 8 out of 10 days or 24 out of 30 days each month and see how well you keep up with everything it takes to manage a household – or in this case, a kingdom. The king and his castle ... I'm away from the castle so much. I had to learn to make the days I'm home as high quality as possible. I had to learn to make long-distance friendships. I had to learn to trust the managers and people in charge of my affairs while I was traveling. Whatever ended up done, or not done, would still have my name on it. So I learned to forgive. Forgiveness is actually a gift to yourself. Many doctors have linked being unforgiving to the development of "dis-ease" in the physical body. Sometimes we hurt others intentionally; more often than not it's unintentional. Many times it's a matter of perception. Sometimes we don't know what we don't know about a situation. Stephen Covey tells a story about a man on a train with several children who are out of control, making all kinds of noise, and basically bothering everyone around them. This man was quite annoyed as you can imagine, grumbling to himself and getting ready to say something to the father who apparently did not care about keeping his kids in line. The father notices the man's growing concern and quietly apologizes. "I'm sorry my kids are acting this way. I'm sure it's frustrating to you. I just don't have the heart to say anything today. You see, we just came from their mother's funeral." That man learned something about perception that day.

I have made up my mind and heart to settle all those kinds of things. I've been forgiven so many things, it is a joy to release others. Once you let go of it, God can do something with it. He restores and makes all things new. Even relationships.

You might think I have no idea what you're going through. Maybe you think I've never had any real pain like you do. Believe me, I've already said that joy is not the absence of adversity. It is the victorious way through adversity. I've been stabbed in the back figuratively and literally. You can see the scar on my back to this day. I did a lot of intentional fouls before I found the Lord. There were plenty of challenges and conflicts along the way. I was quick to defend myself back then. I wasn't the biggest guy on the court and I needed to make sure I didn't get pushed around. As it stands now, it's been many years since I've made any intentional fouls.

As far as I'm concerned, everyone I know has a clean slate to work from. If there's ever been any hurt or offense between me and you – would you forgive me? I've already forgiven you if you've hurt me in any way, or my family.

After my time with the Globetrotters, I wore the uniform of my team, the Shooting Stars.

Everybody gets a clean slate. No house, or business, or fortune is more important to me than good relationships. For me to walk my journey living a life of joy, I need to make sure my focus is on the future, and that the memories of my past that I choose to remember are all the good things (there are so many). I'm thankful and grateful for the opportunity to grow in wisdom and character.

After I accepted Jesus in my life, I began to think about all of God's children as my brothers and sisters. I ministered, I counseled, I testified to the importance of my faith. The Bible says that "we are snared by the words of our mouth." What we say will come back to us, good for good, and bad for bad. If we foul people with our words and actions, those fouls will return to us.

So even though I may have disappointed someone, or offended someone with something I've said, I haven't made an intentional foul for many years.

It's an easy rule to follow. When life throws challenges and frustrations in your path, take them head-on with patience and grace. A few fouls are likely to happen along the way. Just don't commit intentional fouls.

"If you're going

through hell,

keep going."

– Winston Churchill

Chapter 17

Rebounding

Another important part of living a life of joy is being able to rebound.

In basketball, a rebound is gaining control of a missed shot. When a shooter misses a shot, it usually bounces off the rim or the backboard, and then several players jump and push and scramble to grab control of the rebound. It's a very valuable part of the game. When you get a rebound, you're taking away another chance for your opponent to score and creating a new chance for your own team to score.

My one-time Globetrotter teammate, Wilt Chamberlain, has the career record for most rebounds in the NBA – 23,924. That's a lot of rebounds! That means that almost 24,000 times, he captured a missed shot and gave his team another chance to score. Probably on most of those rebounds, he had to wrestle the ball away from several other players who were going after it, too.

Now, it didn't hurt that Wilt was 7'1" tall! He also had great timing, great body positioning, HUGE hands, and an attitude that every ball belonged to him.

That's tenacity. Coaches sometimes call it "want-to" or will.

On the Globetrotters, rebounding was not my primary role. I gathered in my share of missed shots, however my main job was to be the comedian, the passer, and sometimes the shooter. I'm probably about 20,000 rebounds behind Wilt!

In my life outside of basketball, I've had to rebound a lot of times!

In life, rebounding means coming back from adversity, recovering from missed shots, regaining control after a challenging situation. It means bouncing back from something that has knocked you down. It means recovering your joy. You see, when true adversity comes along, happiness is a wimp. Happiness will run away and hide. Joy is something more and something far greater than happiness. Joy is one of the "fruits of the spirit" that are described in Galatians in the Bible, along with love, peace, patience, kindness, goodness, faithfulness, gentleness and self-control.

It is important to choose to look for the good in every situation, to see what can be learned. Think on the good things. Believe that somehow everything will work out for the best. The joy is in knowing and believing. Your mind will be open to new possibilities.

Just as rebounding is an important part of the game of basketball, it's an important part of life. The better you are at rebounding, the more you'll enjoy the game!

I was honored to be enshrined with a great class in the Hall of Fame. Class of 2003 - (l to r) Leon Barmore, Francis D. "Chic" Hearn (his wife Marge Hearn accepted award) Meadowlark Lemon, Earl Lloyd, James Worthy, Robert Parish, Dino Meneghin.

Chapter 18

Free Throws

How many basketball games do you suppose are won or lost at the free-throw line? Probably hundreds every year.

A free throw is just what its name implies. It is an uncontested, unguarded shot from a line 15 feet from the basket. The clock doesn't run. Players get to shoot free throws after they have been fouled by an opposing player, or when the opposing team goes over its limit of fouls. Sometimes, you even get to shoot a free throw when a player or a coach has said the "magic words" to a referee! That's a technical foul, and for some reason, those free throws seem extra sweet.

I'm surrounded by the crew from the *Best Damn Sports Show Period*.

A free throw is free! If it's free, why would you miss?

Good free-throw shooters will make at least 8 out of 10. It should be a relatively easy shot. You have 10 seconds to shoot and no one is guarding you. You're only 15 feet away from the hoop. Contrary to popular belief it's much harder than it looks.

The art of shooting free throws relies as much on practice as on talent. Making them is as much mental as physical. Focus and toughness are the keys, especially when you're standing at the free-throw line for two shots and your team is behind by one point with 2 seconds left in the game. That's when those 15 feet seem like 50.

Rick Barry, who played in the ABA and NBA in the 1960s and 1970s, is the best free-throw shooter in my book. He made 5,713 out of 6,397 in his career, for 89.3 percent. Mark Price is the NBA record holder. He made 90.4 percent of his free throws, even though he only shot about a third as many as did Barry. And since he's my friend, and one of my favorites, I have to mention Calvin Murphy, another free-throw superstar. In one season he sank 206 of 215 free throws.

I shot thousands of free throws in my career. I made 98% of my free throws, so I think I would be called an expert.

I also understand a thing or two about making the kinds of free throws that life gives to us.

I believe that a free throw, in life, is about taking those shots that come free and easily to you. Taking advantage of situations and opportunities that call on you to use your most natural talents.

All of us are blessed with a couple of things that we do better than anybody else. We have natural, inherent talents and gifts. God has given each one of us a world-class talent of some kind.

So shooting a free throw is seeking out those opportunities where it's natural and easy for us to succeed. If you are going to get something for free, then why you gonna miss it?

I've missed more than 9,000 shots in my career. I've lost almost 300 games. Twenty-six times, I've been trusted to take the game-winning shot and missed. I've failed over and over and over again in my life. And that is why I succeed."

– Michael Jordan

Chapter
19

3-Point Shots

Many years ago, the Globetrotters invented long-range shooting. I'm going on the record here, it is a fact that Abe Saperstein, yours truly Meadowlark Lemon, and the Harlem Globetrotters invented the three point shot. We had players who could make 8-for-10 or even 9-for-10 from way outside today's 3-point line. If you couldn't make 7-for-10 as a Globetrotter, you weren't allowed to take that shot in a game. I was shooting 7-for-10 from half court, and my hook shot from long range was like a free throw to me!

A lot of the players who tried out with the Globetrotters couldn't believe how we could all shoot from way out. I wonder what our scoring averages would have been if those long shots we were sinking would have counted for three points instead of two.

So after we had perfected the long shot, the old American Basketball Association, and later the NBA and the college game, incorporated the 3-point shot as an official rule. A big arc painted on the court above the key and down into the corners became "3-point country." If a player made a shot from beyond this arc, it counted for three points, not the usual two.

Taking this long shot has proved hard to resist for modern players. In the last several years, teams began to fire up dozens of 3-pointers per game. Shooting percentages went down because it's hard to shoot with great accuracy from more than 20 feet out. The reward outweighs most of the risk. Just look at Reggie Miller.

Reggie Miller, that long, lanky shooter for the Indianapolis Pacers for many years, leads the NBA with the most 3-point shots ever made: 2,560. He took 6,486 3-point shots and made 2,560, which works out to about a 40 percent success rate. (That would have been nothing for Marques Haynes, Curly Neal, Hallie Bryant, or Wally Choice, just to name a few of the Globetrotters.)

Now, a lot of people would say 40% is not too good. Look at it this way: most players are going to take only two-point shots. If they shoot 50% out of every 100 shots – which would be considered very good – they would score 100 points. Reggie, and the other 3-point sharpshooters, would score 120 points by making only 40% of 100 shots.

High risk, high reward. And the courage to stand out of the crowd and take a bigger risk.

What does all this have to do with a life of joy? Well, I think our lives would get pretty boring if we shot only layups. It gives us freedom to put up 3-pointers every once in a while. Go ahead and take a risk. You might miss the shot. Stay positive. If it does go in, it's worth more!

Will Rogers had a saying I've always liked: "Go out on a limb. That's where the fruit is."

I have taken many risks in my life. The biggest was leaving the comfort of home, Wilmington, North Carolina, for a try-out with the Globetrotters. I have also taken risks by starting up other comedy basketball teams, like The Shooting Stars, The Bucketeers and the Harlem All-Stars.

I have started youth basketball camps, my charitable foundation, and the Meadowlark Lemon Ministries, just to name a few of my ventures. Although those are sources of joy to me, they came with some risk. What in life doesn't involve some risk?

We think we're safe and secure because we stick to our own little corner of the world. Maybe we live in the same house, and drive the same car until the wheels fall off.

Maybe we put as much money as we can into a savings account for a "rainy day."

By doing these things, we think we're taking the risk out of our lives. That's a false reality.

Life is not entirely controllable. We can't always manage it perfectly. So why not live it? Live it strong and take the right shot! And that means shooting a 3-pointer every once in a while. Go ahead and apply for that job you're interested in. It may not turn out exactly like you want. How do you know if you don't risk it? Go ahead and ask that girl out to dinner. Maybe all you'll end up with is a good meal, who knows ... Maybe you'll end up with a lover for life.

If you feel you've lost your way spiritually, why not attend a worship service at the church around the corner. You might just find something – or someone – to lift you up.

Every time I threw up that half-court hook shot at the end of a Globetrotters game, some thought I was risking that it might not go in. Some thought there was a risk that I would get laughed at for the wrong reason or that some family who had come to watch us play might have to go home and tell their friends that Meadowlark missed that day.

But I shot it every time. And there was no risk to me. *I knew* it was going in. Everyone held their breath. And it was a thrill every time regardless of the outcome.

Another thing. These days, that hook shot would have counted for *three* points.

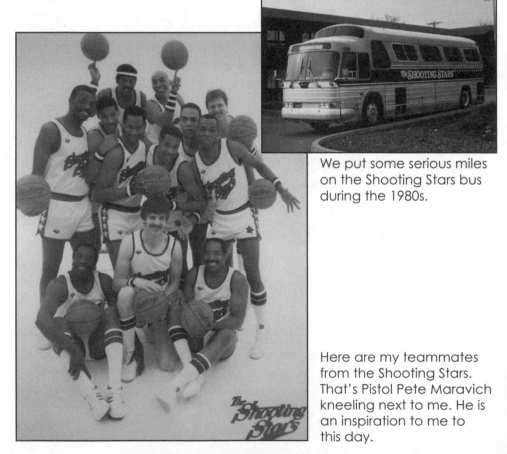

We put some serious miles on the Shooting Stars bus during the 1980s.

Here are my teammates from the Shooting Stars. That's Pistol Pete Maravich kneeling next to me. He is an inspiration to me to this day.

The person who risks nothing, does nothing, has nothing, is nothing, and becomes nothing. He may avoid suffering and sorrow, but he simply cannot learn and feel and change and grow and love and live."

– Leo F. Buscaglia

It takes many good deeds to build a good reputation, and only one bad one to lose it."

– Benjamin Franklin

"Defending Your Good Name"

"A good name is more desirable than great riches; to be esteemed is better than silver or gold." (Proverbs 22:1)

My given name is Meadow Lemon III. My dad, Peanut Lemon, was Meadow II and his dad was the first Meadow. My son is the fourth and his son, my grandson, is the fifth.

I'm the one and only Meadowlark! The name has always suited me. The birds named meadowlark are known for their sweet and happy songs. And I always tried to put a song in the hearts of my fans.

Meadowlark became my "brand" name with the Globetrotters and, over the years, it became the only name anybody knew me by.

On the television game show "Who Wants to Be a Millionaire?" the host asked contestants on several occasions: Who is the Clown Prince of Basketball? My name was the correct answer that no one ever missed!

Back in 1982, I topped the "Q" poll as most popular athlete. That's a poll that measures the name recognition and popularity of celebrities, politicians, brand names, and products.

There are some other well known people who go by a single name: Elvis, Madonna, Pelé, Cher, and the man who changed my life named Jesus.

Here I am with Shaq. We participated in the 2010 Albert Pujols Family Foundation Celebrity Golf Tournament.

One of my greatest compliments is when people who I admire, and are superstars in their own right, refer to me as their hero or inspiration.

For example, another guy people know by just the one name – Shaq – Shaquille O'Neal, saw me in the audience during a game and shouted over to me: "Meet me in the locker room after the game." This was during a game, mind you. So I went down to the dressing room afterwards, and Shaq said to me, "When I was a little kid, you autographed a picture of yourself for me. I don't know what became of it. It got lost somewhere along the line. Would you sign another one for me?"

The picture and the memories still mean a lot to Shaq even though he's a superstar himself! It makes me wonder how many other kids did I encourage with just a random act of kindness, with a word of encouragement or a smile or selecting them out of a crowd of people to be part of what I was doing.

Most times we never know what these acts of kindness have produced. Other times, we find out in the most amazing ways.

Isaiah Thomas, the Hall of Fame guard, came up to me in an airport recently while I was on the phone. Isaiah got on his knees in front of me and looked up toward me and said thank you for what you did for me and so many of us who have become NBA players. Then he got up and continued on to catch his flight.

Another time, Charles Barkley, Hall of Famer and popular TV broadcaster, looked at me while we were on the Phoenix Suns private plane traveling to a game and said, "Meadowlark, every one of us on this team got something from you … we all wanted to be like you when we were growing up!"

James Worthy (HOF 2003) told me his dad used to bring him out to watch me play when we would go to Charlotte, North Carolina. He thanked me for playing. I see his championship rings with the Lakers, and that is more than enough thanks. Even Dino Meneghin (HOF 2003) said he saw me play in Italy, in the small town where he lived, and he wanted to play center because he saw me playing the pivot. Sure enough, he played center, and grew to be 7 feet tall. You never know who is watching you. You never know when inspiration will strike. I'm honored these two were enshrined in the Hall of Fame in my class of 2003.

Things like that happen to me from time to time, so a lot of people ask me, "Why is that? How have you kept your "good name" through all these years?"

I think the best way to answer that question is: have respect. Have respect for yourself and for the people who brought you into this world and for all the people of this world.

In order to be respected by others, you first have to respect yourself. The great Jackie Robinson once said,

"I'm not concerned with your liking or disliking me ...
All I ask is that you respect me as a human being."

Jackie had to have incredible respect for himself, and for the situation that history put him in as the first black player to cross the color line of Major League Baseball. Besides self-respect, he needed unbelievable courage.

I had to develop my own self-respect and character when I was a little black kid in the South. I had to overcome the feeling of being inferior when I was forced to drink out of certain drinking fountains or sit in the back of the bus. When the world you're living in gives you no sign of respect or self-worth or value, then you have to create it for yourself.

Believe me, that's not easy. And I feel sad because I think a lot of people today are trapped in lives of poverty and crime because they were never able to develop self-respect.

So respect is a key part of keeping a good name for yourself.

In a book, I can only talk the talk. It's more important to "walk the walk." I had alcohol just the one time in high school and I hated it so much I never drank it again. Besides, it is important to me to keep my body healthy, and that stuff doesn't have anything to do with good health!

I don't think it would have been right for a person as famous and visible as me to embrace such things. People held me to a higher standard, and I tried very hard to live up to that standard. I hold *myself* to a high standard. I always expect more of myself than anyone expects of me.

Kids look up to me. I want them to be able to say, "Look at Meadowlark. Look at how he conducts himself and the standards he has created for himself. If he can do it, I can, too."

People have told me that I have been an inspiration to them because of my authenticity. I try to genuinely be who I am, all the time. No fakes. No hidden ball tricks.

The ability to fake well in basketball and leave the man guarding you grasping at air is very helpful. In life, you need to play it straight-up.

Your name is valuable. The value of your name is in direct proportion to your character. The formula is simple. Attaining it takes work. Good character, good name. Bad character, bad name. We receive a name at birth, and then spend our entire lives attaching meaning to it. We know plenty of people who have built great value around their names. Most of the time if you mention the name, people will remember something about that person's character.

When a company or corporation's value is calculated, they study their assets and liabilities, productivity and market share – as well as the value of their good name.

A good name is priceless. It's because it's so difficult to earn a good name and reputation, and it's so easy to lose. A person can spend a lifetime working to gain a solid reputation – a good name – for having integrity and honesty and fairness. Tell one lie, make one unethical compromise, make an unreasonable decision, and then what? You don't get free throws in life for that, buddy.

You start by looking at how you behave. My wife and I tell our kids, "You represent our family when you are out and about so **get caught doing good.**" Part of having a good name happens when we are careful with the reputation of others. This is no time to live like no one else matters. That's a quick way to squander your life. If you have a conversation or argument with a neighbor, keep it between the two of you. Don't betray another man's confidence, or the person who hears it may shame you and you will never lose a bad reputation.

I am who I am. What you see is what you get. I don't have a public side and a different private side. I'm the same Meadowlark on Monday as I am on Friday. I'm the same Meadowlark in the morning as I am late at night. I'm the same Meadowlark in the privacy of my home with Cynthia and the kids and the grandkids as I am in front of a big audience in an auditorium. I am the person God made.

The past few years, I've been doing a lot of missionary work with Native Americans. As part of that work, a Dakota tribe has given me a special name. Their name for me is Ta-She-Ya-Ka – their word for Meadowlark. In their tongue, it means "bird chirping, reminding people to get up."

I love this name. I like to think about the meaning this way: I have spent most of my life reminding people to get UP! To be positive. Energetic. Hopeful. Enthusiastic. You know, UP! Ready to take on the world with as much joy as we can muster.

So it's a fitting name for me, and it says something about my soul at a deep level.

A wise person once said, "The authentic self is the soul made visible." Man, I think that says it all. If you let your real character shine through in all that you do and with everyone you meet, people will see that. They will be able to see the real you. I've always felt happy and blessed to be me, so why not let that come through?

We like to think that we can "fake it." We're good actors and actresses. And we might just win an Academy Award and "fool" someone. Once. Maybe twice. Not for long.

Being our most authentic, soulful selves is the best thing to do, because we're going to do it whether we mean to or not!

If you're constantly changing who you are to make yourself feel comfortable in different situations, you're just chasing happiness. You'll never catch it until you stop long enough to capture your own character and figure out a way to let it be the only "you."

Our friends and family can help us. Counseling can help. And I believe spending time with Jesus – just your heart with his, one-on-one, together – can help, too.

So, keeping your "good name" has to do with respect, walking the talk, and with showing your character.

One other thing about Defending Your Good Name ... make yourself unique. Make yourself someone who is easy for others to remember. Create a "brand name" for yourself.

I know a man who works as a life coach to college football and basketball coaches during their off-seasons. He meets with them one-on-one to discuss whatever they need help with – not in leading their athletic teams – rather in living their lives. With some, he helps them with time management and striking a healthy work-life balance. With others, he works on their self-confidence and helping them understand their roles as educators, not just as people who show kids the Xs and Os.

He calls himself "The Coaches' Coach." Those are powerful words to put on your business card. It clearly describes who he is and what he loves to do.

With me, I am a basketball-playing comedian, or a comedian who plays basketball. I'm not sure which. And I'm not sure it matters much. The point is that I'm unique. There aren't many people runnin' around with those credentials.

So, think about how to make yourself unique. Come up with a short description that's easy to remember, like the "Coaches' Coach." And start puttin' it out there as an important statement of who you are.

It will help you defend your good name.

Last point. I won't say I've been perfect at defending my reputation my whole life. As a younger man, I made plenty of mistakes. I had to try on some different roles before I figured out who I really was and who I was meant to be. I would tell you I've had more joy ever since I started walking down the true path that was set before me.

I want you to find your path and walk it with strength, and with courage, and with respect for yourself and for others. Walk it every day in every way. It will fill you with joy, and it will keep you from committing those intentional fouls.

*"You don't build a reputation
by what you are going to do ...
it is what you are doing
and by what you've done."*

– Henry Ford

"Don't make a

million-dollar

move and a

10-cent finish."

– Michael Jordan

Chapter 21

Finishing Strong

Technically, I am ageless. I like to say that I have not gotten old. I have just gotten older! I take good care of myself. I know I still have a lot of important work left to do. In a lot of ways, I feel like I'm just getting started.

When someone asks me how old I am, I laugh. "I'm ageless." It's not about the number; there is an ageless quality to being healthy. When I make healthy choices every day, I restore my body instead of allowing it to deteriorate. I prevent and restore. Disease is not something that automatically accompanies aging.

You can retire from your job. You should never retire from life.

Sadly, a lot of people don't retire ... they just *stop*. They might feel tired, used up. They might feel like it's time for younger people to carry the weight of the world, or like it's someone else's turn to take on the big problems of the day.

We all know someone like this. They might tell you they are happy to just be pokin' around in their garden or catching up on their reading. It's usually easy to tell that something is missing in their life. Something to propel them forward. Something to help them finish strong.

They say, "It's too late for me. I've had my chances already." I say it's never too late – God will always give you another chance. As long as you have breath and you're alive, you have a purpose.

Graveyards are full of people who had great "unused" talents and potential. They were afraid to develop them – to step out and take a chance. They were always waiting for the "right time" when everything was perfect. They never focused on perfect practice.

If you have a dream to be a great piano player and you buy a piano and put it in your room and never play it – you just look at it and dream about one day playing that piano professionally – it will never happen. Dreams have to be followed with action. You need piano lessons and practice, and with time you will develop.

My message is "Life's Most Meaningless Statistic Is the Halftime Score." It's about making the most of your God-given gifts ... no matter how old you are or how much you feel you've already accomplished.

Some people feel that they've climbed to the top of the mountain at a fairly young age. There are company CEOs who make millions of dollars at the age of 40. There are actors and entertainers and music stars who become world-famous by the age of 20!

There are young basketball players out there today who haven't even thought about being 40 years old yet! They can only think about today or tomorrow, maybe. They don't give a thought to their future out there in the distance.

I have put no limit on how long I'll keep playing and entertaining fans. I used to say that in five years, if I've done what I want to do, I'll be fine with that. I keep adding years to it. I'll probably keep going until Jesus comes and tells me it's time to go with him for my next game.

Moses lived to be way over 100 years old. If God did it for Moses, why not for you? Why not me, too? I feel as good as Moses was described. It was said, "His eyes were not dim and his vigor was not diminished." He was ageless.

I'm wearing the uniform of my current team, Meadowlark Lemon's Harlem All-Stars™.

I think everyone should promise to do at least three things in their later years. These will help you get not old, just older.

1. Take good care of your health through exercise and proper nutrition. Get up and do something. Start where you are, use what you have, do what you can.

2. Learn something new. You don't know everything yet. Keep your mind working.

3. Share your wisdom. Whether you're 11 or 120, life has taught you many valuable lessons. Pass what you know along to others. Be sure to give the gift of your experiences and wisdom to others. It's a way of paying back those who did it for us.

My longtime friend Madeline Mims is a great example of finishing strong. She is a four-time Olympic gold and silver medalist. She knows about overcoming obstacles. When she was three years old, she had spinal meningitis and wasn't expected to live. The doctors said she would never be normal, mentally or physically. God had a plan for her life. She had a mother who prayed for her through those years. It produced out of her weakness a mindset of fight and drive and a never-give-up attitude that a champion needs.

She was one of the first female American middle distance stars of world-class caliber. Madeline was the 1968 Olympic 800 meter champion. From 1967 to 1980, she won 10 national indoor and outdoor titles and set numerous American records.

Her 1968 Olympic victory was unexpected and decisive, as she won by more than 10 meters in an Olympic record of 2:00.9. She also was a member of the 1972 and 1976 Olympic teams and in 1980, at the age of 32, won the U.S. Olympic Trials. Only the U.S. boycott of the Moscow Games kept her out of her fourth Olympiad. Coming out of retirement three times during her career, she also won a silver medal at the 1972 Olympic Games as a member of the 4 x 400 meter relay team.

Madeline finished strong at the Olympics and continues her journey today by mentoring and training others to finish strong!

My friend Bob Wieland has an incredible, inspirational story. So much so, he is famously called "Mr. Inspiration." He is well-known to many Americans for his role on NBC's weekly series *Sonny Spoon* and his appearances on ABC's *Wide World of Sports*. He is a true American hero, who is a beacon of hope for anyone who has a dream, a goal, and a desire to achieve all that they can in their life. While serving our country in

Vietnam, Bob lost both of his legs in a near–fatal accident with a land mine.

Bob did not let that accident and the loss of his legs defeat him. He found a way to overcome that injury, and he turned it into something that could help others. He returned to the United States to overcome all odds and he became a champion weight lifter, marathon runner, triathlete, motivational speaker, and television actor. He has become an advocate for those who have no voice ... for those who are homeless, hungry, and spiritually lost.

In 1982, he walked across America to raise money for the Red Cross and other relief organizations. He began his long journey in California; with padded knuckles, he traveled 4,900,016 steps and it took him three and a half years. Even after everyone left him, he finished strong! He completed his journey at the base of the Vietnam Memorial in Washington, D.C., where he placed a wreath by the name of the man whose life he had tried to save in Vietnam when Bob lost his legs. President Ronald Reagan was there to congratulate him on finishing strong on his journey across America. Bob's philosophy is: "Nothing is impossible with God!" He is a living example of that!

Life is not about a time limit. It's about completion. It's not about age. We are ageless.

We get better every day as we labor at our task at hand. Somewhere in the future, I see us looking better than we look right now. In light of the possible storms facing our country and the world, it's never been more important to lay aside our differences, laugh together, take a stand together, forgive one another. From the age of 11, I have focused on what I do have to work with instead of on what I don't have. Be creative. This is how inventions are made. Make your own basket if you have to.

Remember that finishing strong has nothing to do with age. A very young soldier at age 18, 19, or 20 goes through special training to learn the skills that assist him or her to make quick, life-altering decisions in the face of danger. They are compelled to acquire wisdom at an early age. When they enlist in the military, they are making a choice to be in situations where they may be required to give their life for another – they finish strong. Many individuals have short lives and yet the life they lived was significant to the quality of another's life.

A friend of mine had a brother who died about seven years ago at age 17 when he was in a car accident that was not his fault. He had made a decision to be an organ donor at a time when he expected to live to be much, much older. My friend and his family have communicated with the people who have received his brother's eyes, heart, liver, and other vital organs and, when possible, have actually met with the beneficiaries of this precious young man's life saving organs. The wisdom and foresight to become an organ donor when he was just a teenager has now brought sight and health and life to others, and comfort and joy to the family he left behind. They are comforted when they see the joy and blessing their son's life has brought to another.

Jesus accomplished so much in a short time. Jesus understood this. He had 30 quiet years, then three and a half years of finishing strong!

John the Baptist had about 30 quiet, preparatory years, then about one year of fruitful ministry until his death. He finished strong!

Many people's lives have been cut short. They did not have the luxury of learning wisdom through their life's experiences to become wise in their older years. There are many examples of older people who have no sense at all. Instead of gaining wisdom through the years, they have just gotten more foolish. A person can be 90 years old and still be ignorant; they could live their whole life in error. A person could have a pure heart and just have an ignorant part of their brain. Wisdom can be more abundant in a 15-year-old than in a 90-year-old. We should all seek knowledge; there is always something we don't know.

Wisdom and significance are not just things that naturally accompany aging. If you always do what you've always done, you will always get the same results. In order to change and get better, you have to choose to learn new ways of doing things, get new information, seek out new things, change your location, change something or everything, get started in a new direction. One step at a time – one day at a time becomes one month and then one year.

Pursuing something is a sign of passion. Destiny is not inevitable; it's a possibility. We are required to participate in our destiny.

When we are focused on a goal – a possibility in our future – it keeps us from thinking about the past. Being successful along the way gives us confidence to keep moving toward our goal. That could mean we can do one push-up for three days and by the end of the week we're up to five push-ups. By the end of the second week, we're up to 12 push-ups and on it goes until we reach our goal of 50 push-ups. This can be applied to weight loss or anything that requires a starting point on our way to the finishing line. Keep at your goal with the same enthusiasm you started with.

It's been said by researches that we are only six people away from any human on earth. It's called the human web or 6 degrees of separation. God can get you anywhere he wants you in a day. In a single day, God can change your world.

Today, I am a totally different person from what I was before I met the man who changed my life, Jesus Christ. I know without a doubt that I am a person with a spirit/soul on the inside that will never die. I believe that the body dies and the spirit/soul lives forever. I think differently now than I did before my experience with the Lord. I always have a joyful connection with my audience and playing basketball games is a joy to me. Ministering to people also is a joy to me.

My goal is practicing forgiveness in advance. I decide before I get out of bed that I am going to treat everyone I meet with respect, love, and forgiveness, as if they were a newborn baby, whether they are a family member or a clerk in a store or even a guy who cuts me off in traffic. If someone cuts me off in traffic, I may have an initial feeling of anger toward that person. Then I quickly remember that I choose to live in forgiveness and I let that feeling of anger go. In the past, I may have let that incident bother me for days or weeks. Now, I just drive.

Success in life is not measured by how fast we sprint away from the starting line. No! Victory is won by running the full race, finishing strong, and crossing the finish line.

Make up your mind to finish strong. It has been said that it matters less where you begin in life than where you end up. I believe this statement has merit. Remember: it requires strict training, not the path of least resistance.

Life can be likened to a race or a game with a definite beginning, a definite end, and a whole lot of time in the middle where people jockey for position. As long as you are still in the race, there's a chance you will win. Take yourself out of the game and it's certain you will lose.

One significant difference between life and any other game or race is that in life we only compete against ourselves. Even though others may be involved, each person's life is judged by no greater criteria than how they did when measured against their own individual potential.

Decide right now that you are going to begin a new chapter in your life. Why wait until January 1 to make your resolution? Make your declaration today and finish this day strong, this week strong, this month strong, this year strong.

Victory and success begin with a decision and they gain strength through the daily declaration of our faith in God's future for our life.

The Bible is a book of true life stories in which people, despite the hardships of life, finish strong because of their faith in God.

You can be one of God's success stories ... ask him to help you and he will. Get on God's side and finish strong.

My son, do not forget my teaching,
 but keep my commands in your heart,
for they will prolong your life many years
 and bring you prosperity.
Let love and faithfulness never leave you;
 bind them around your neck,
 write them on the tablet of your heart.
Then you will win favor and a good name
 in the sight of God and man.

Proverbs 3

"Kindness is
more than deeds.
It is an attitude,
an expression, a
look, a touch.
It is anything
that lifts another
person."

– Unknown

Chapter
22

The Final Score

The final chapter is not yet written in my life. I don't know the final score, although you'd better believe I am showing up to see what the score is!

I think we should count the number of loving family members we have, and the number of caring friends. I think we should "keep score" by the number of wonderful experiences we've had. Experiences become a part of you. I'll always remember all the wonderful places I've been fortunate enough to travel through and all the wonderful people who I have met along the way, and you have become part of me.

I believe I'll see with my own eyes the goodness of the Lord working in my children's lives. I want my kids and their kids to have Godly, healthy, and long lives. I want them to respect themselves and others, and to be grateful for their blessings. I want you to always remember that I said life's most meaningless statistic is the half time score, and as far as I'm concerned it's always half time.

You know, I bet nobody ever remembered the final score of a Globetrotters' game. If 10,000 people came to a Globetrotter game, I bet not 10 of them could tell you the actual score of the game. It simply didn't matter.

It's the joy that counts in life. Not the points, not the things, not the stuff. Be excited about the future. You're going to spend the rest of your life there. The common denominator for all mankind is that we all get 24 hours in a day, just like everyone else. What you do with that time is up to you. Choose well. Don't worry about the final score. God is on His throne. The best is yet to come.

And isn't this the ultimate score? God 1, You 1. A one-on-one relationship with our Creator for all eternity.

I wish you *joy,* my friends.

"Breathe.
Let go.
And remind
yourself that
this very
moment is the
only one you
know you have
for sure."

– Oprah Winfrey

Appendices

---◆---

Official Biography in the Naismith Memorial Basketball Hall of Fame

Meadowlark Lemon

Enshrined 2003
Wilmington, N.C.

"**F**ew athletes in any sport have impacted their sport on a worldwide level more than Meadowlark Lemon. Perhaps the most well-known and beloved member of the Harlem Globetrotters, Lemon played in more than 16,000 games in a career that began with the Globetrotters in 1955 and still continues with Meadowlark Lemon's Harlem All Stars ™. Known as the "Clown Prince of Basketball," Lemon's favored "can't-miss" half-court hook shot and comedic routines entertained millions of fans in more than 94 countries around the globe.

---◆---

Official Biography in the Naismith Memorial Basketball Hall of Fame

Harlem Globetrotters

Enshrined 2002

In basketball's storied history, there may be no single organization more synonymous with the game than the world-famous Harlem Globetrotters. Originally formed from the Wendell Phillips High School, the team played in the Negro American Legion League as the "Giles Post," and turned professional as the Savoy Big Five. Promoter and future Hall of Famer Abe Saperstein bought the team and re-named it the Harlem Globetrotters. Up until the late 1930s, the Globetrotters were a serious competitive team, and in 1940 won the prestigious World Professional Basketball Tournament in Chicago. With the acquisition of Inman Jackson in 1939, the Globetrotters began to work more light entertainment and comedic routines into their appearances. After World War II, the team became real "globetrotters," traveling the world and entertaining thousands. With players such as Geese Ausbie, Goose Tatum, Marques Haynes, Curly Neal and Meadowlark Lemon, the Globetrotters became basketball ambassadors, bringing their showmanship and goodwill to millions. The team remains as popular as ever.

———— ♦ ————

John W. Bunn Award
Meadowlark Lemon was the Bunn honoree in 2000.

The John W. Bunn Award is named for the first chairman of the Basketball Hall of Fame Committee (1949-69). The award, instituted by the Hall's Board of Trustees, annually honors an international or national figure who has contributed greatly to the game of basketball. Outside of Enshrinement, the John W. Bunn Award is the most prestigious award presented by the Basketball Hall of Fame.

———— ♦ ————

In 1975, Meadowlark Lemon was inducted into the North Carolina Sports Hall of Fame.
The following citation accompanied his enshrinement:
Meadowlark Lemon, 1975

Member of the Harlem Globetrotters, 1955–1980, 1993. All-state basketball and football player at Williston High School, 1952. Enrolled at Florida A&M in 1952 and was drafted by U.S. Army. Discharged in 1954, joining the Globetrotters the following year. An unusually skilled ball handler and natural comedian, he proved one of the most popular Globetrotters. Became known as the Clown Prince of Basketball.

◆

Meadowlark received his Globetrotters "Legends" Ring and had his jersey (No. 36) retired as part of a 75th anniversary charity fund-raiser on January 5, 2001, at Chicago's Fairmont Hotel.

Here is the list of Globetrotters' retired jerseys:
- 13: Wilt Chamberlain; March 9, 2000
- 20: Marques Haynes; January 5, 2001
- 36: Meadowlark Lemon; January 5, 2001
- 50: Reece "Goose" Tatum; February 8, 2002
- 22: Fred "Curly" Neal; February 15, 2008

◆

Meadowlark was the recipient of the International Clown Hall Of Fame Lifetime of Laughter Award in 2000.

I've always loved to clown around.

———————◆———————

In January 1997, Meadowlark was honored with the Sports Legends Award at *Ebony* magazine's 50th anniversary. Also in that class of honorees were boxing legend Muhammad Ali, Olympic sprinter Florence Griffith-Joyner, and baseball immortal Jackie Robinson.

I was so proud to join Muhammad Ali, Florence Griffith-Joyner, Jim Brown, and Rachel Robinson, Jackie Robinson's widow, on the stage at *Ebony's* 50th Anniversary celebration, We were introduced by Bill Cosby, comic TV star and occasional Globetrotter.

———————◆———————

In 2006, Meadowlark was honored with a star on the Celebrate Wilmington! Walk of Fame. The walk recognizes Wilmingtonians who have attained national and international fame in their field.

For More Information About Meadowlark Lemon, Refer to the Following Books:

The Ultimate Encyclopedia of Basketball – Referenced on page 11
Smith, Ron. *Ultimate Encyclopedia of Basketball*. Carlton Books Limited, 1996, 1996.
ISBN: 1- 85868- 151-0

Best by Number: Who wore what, with distinction – Referenced on page 120
Sporting News. *Best by Number.* Sporting News Publishing Co., 2006. 120.
ISBN: 0-89204-848-4

America's Athletes – Referenced on page 75
Tenuto, Sandra. *America's Athletes.* FairPlay Foundation, 2003. 75.
ISBN: N/A

Sports Illustrated - The Basketball Book – Referenced on page 208
Wolff, Alexander, Rob Fleder, and Jack McCallum. *Sports Illustrated, The Basketball Book.* Sports Illustrated, 2007, 208
ISBN: 1-933821-19-1

Basketball Legends of All Times – Referenced on pages 116 & 117
Rousso, Nick. *Basketball Legends of All Times.* Publications International, Ltd.
Library of Congress Catalog Card Number: 96-70261
1996
ISBN: 0-7853-1965-4

Hoops Heaven: Commemorating the 50th Anniversary of the Naismith Memorial Basketball Hall of Fame – Referenced on page 93.
Ascend Books, LLC 2009.
ISBN: 978-0-9817166-8-8

A portion of proceeds from the sale of
Trust Your Next Shot benefits the following charities:

———————◆———————

The Smile of a Child:

The mission of Smile of a Child is to provide spiritual ministry
to people around the world by providing humanitarian assistance to the physical,
mental, emotional and sometimes financial needs of the individual, thus showing
the love of God and allowing God to manifest himself in a real way in their lives.
Smile of a Child has reached out to needy people around the world who are poor,
hurting, hungry, homeless, orphaned, suffering from physical and sometimes
terminal illness, or who have other needs which can be met through various
humanitarian outreaches provided by this ministry. God's love for all of his
children is limitless and through the humanitarian activities of Smile of a Child,
it is their hope that we not only bring a smile to the face of a child, but
also to open to a door to a personal relationship with Jesus Christ.
www.smileofachild.org

———————◆———————

The ASPCA:

The ASPCA, the **A**merican **S**ociety for the **P**revention of **C**ruelty to **A**nimals, has
a mission making the world a better place for animals. It is particularly involved
concerning animals that are pets or are wild animals being held in captivity.
www.aspca.com

———————◆———————

Festival of Life World Outreach Ministries
"Benefiting Native American Children and their families"

Festival of Life World Outreach Ministries provides compassionate, loving
and competent services in the name of Christ to an often forgotten people.
They have developed programs to provide medicine, toiletries, water, coats,
blankets, food and other essential goods and transportation, and educational
supplies to Indian children and their families in remote areas in California,
Arizona, North and South Dakota, New Mexico. They are continuing
to develop outreaches throughout the United States.
www.folwom.com